T0208434

You Can Know His Voice

The Gospel of Peace

Treva Scott Thompson

WESTBOW
PRESS®
A DIVISION OF THOMAS NELSON
& ZONDERVAN

This book is a work of non-fiction. Unless otherwise noted, the author and the publisher make no explicit guarantees as to the accuracy of the information contained in this book and in some cases, names of people and places have been altered to protect their privacy.

WestBow Press books may be ordered through booksellers or by contacting:

WestBow Press
A Division of Thomas Nelson & Zondervan
1663 Liberty Drive
Bloomington, IN 47403
www.westbowpress.com
844-714-3454

Because of the dynamic nature of the Internet, any web addresses or links contained in this book may have changed since publication and may no longer be valid. The views expressed in this work are solely those of the author and do not necessarily reflect the views of the publisher, and the publisher hereby disclaims any responsibility for them.

Any people depicted in stock imagery provided by Getty Images are models, and such images are being used for illustrative purposes only. Certain stock imagery © Getty Images.

Scripture taken from the King James Version of the Bible.

ISBN: 978-1-6642-1662-4 (sc)
ISBN: 978-1-6642-1663-1 (hc)
ISBN: 978-1-6642-1661-7 (e)

Library of Congress Control Number: 2020924921

Print information available on the last page.

WestBow Press rev. date: 01/11/2021

Dedicated to my children.

My daughter, Joni Lynn Soale: she was helpful and supportive during the writing of this book. Also, to my son, Brent Eugene Soale, and his family.

Contents

Introduction

I first started seeking God to free my mind of the torments I had heard when I attended church as a child.

Almost daily, I searched God for answers. I had a reference Bible and went from one scripture to another. As I studied, I wrote down everything that I had learned. I wrote down my prayers. I wrote down my questions. I wrote down my answers. I wrote down my fears and doubts. I told God about what I felt and why I felt that way. I opened my soul to God. I hid nothing. I sought and prayed until I found His love. It has taken a long time to be freed from the fears and doubts that haunted me.

As I wrote my prayers to God, God began giving me words from Him. As fast as I could write, the words came to me. I did not think of what I would write; the words simply flowed. I was bewildered, and then I remembered the scripture (John 7:37–38,) "If any man thirst, let him come unto me and drink. He that believeth on me; as the scriptures hath said out of his belly shall flow rivers of living water." His words were satisfying my thirst.

All, He gave me was helpful, in understanding His Word. I kept all the writings over the years, have looked back on them, and have continually received help from what I had written. He says His Word would not pass- away. His words are as true today as they were when He comforted me.

Everything He gave me was written in the Bible. There was no conflict, no misunderstanding. They were words of life. They burned inside me. I felt freed for the first time. I knew God was a God of love. He had wooed me with His words of love.

They were words, that Jesus told the people when He walked on earth. "Come unto Me, all ye that labor and are heavy laden, and I will give you rest" (Matthew 11:28).

God has always communicated with His children. Many accept it when it is spoken in the Bible, but they find it hard to believe now. Many say they have a feeling and know it is God. God knows each one of us. He knows how to get our attention. Some people say God speaks to them about a certain problem, through the words of the Bible. God can speak to us, but we need an ear to hear. When we pray, we need to listen for an answer. The answer is sometimes so different than what we expected that we do not accept it as God's Word. We think it is our thinking, our fleshly minds. God is very gentle and never condemning, so we do not always hear Him. There is always a time and season for everything. We know that they who wait on the Lord shall renew their strength.

Some say when they let their Bibles fall open to a certain verse, that is the way God speaks to them.

Many of the blessings from God came through listening to gospel music. His words are just as true in a song as in the Bible. They are praises to him and uplifting to us. Many songs come to me and give me peace and rest. I will find myself humming a song, and maybe I will hum that song for several days. I find out that was exactly what I needed to see me though the conflict I might be confronting. God always comes on time, but that is not always our time.

I needed to think upon things that were edifying, and I heard songs that gave praise to God and songs of blessings from God. When I needed His help, it was right there, ready to be used.

The writings I have compiled are sometimes personal. The words in the Bible can be very personal but can be used by all. His words are no respect of persons.

His words will not pass- away. I cannot allow myself to destroy these writings. I do not know what will be done with them. His words are so alive and can be a blessing and encouragement to one and all. That is why I decided to include these writings I have compiled through the years.

Know that as you seek God's face and get His words written upon your heart and mind, He will use those words to walk and talk with you.

You will always know His words never conflict with the Bible.

They are always comforting and peaceful, without condemnation. He never pressures and is always gently leading.

I have found He shows me the right way to go before He shows me where I was wrong. His love is so gentle and is easily entreated. He will never leave us or forsake us. Take hope.

These words have brought me from a fearful child to a believer who knows God is a good Father and wants the best for His children. He is not tight-fisted with His love and wisdom. His love flows freely; we have only to take hold of His hand with an open mind, knowing He wants the absolute best for us.

He does not settle for less. He sent His Son to bring us back into fellowship with Him. He did not do that in vain. His love is patient, and His mercies are forever.

His words comfort us. He knows what we have need even before we ask for it. Do you know anyone else like that?

Above all, He can be trusted to be the same loving Father each time we walk and talk with Him.

Hopefully, as you read God's words and the following writings, you will give all the glory to our loving Father for His mercy.

1

Praise to God

Dear God, until You gave Your love to me, I had never known love.
I had never felt love until I gave my love to You.
I never felt needed until I needed You.
No one had really seemed to care until I started caring.
No one seemed to look my way until You opened my eyes.
I thought this was a cold, dark world until You lit a flame.
Your hand reached out to help me when I extended mine.

2

Find God

Where have I looked?
Where have I sought?
Where did I have to roam?
How many wakeful nights?
How many days of deep thought?
How many hours of depression?
How many times of frustration, doubt, the tormenting
thoughts, tears, and distress, only to find God?
When I found myself.

3

Made in God's Image

God breathed the life of His spirit into me, made me a living soul, and never left me.

The preaching I heard made me think I was not good enough to have God as my Father.

Then as I studied God's Word, I realized the only sin I was born with was the sin of unbelief. The sin that Jesus came and suffered on the cross to cleanse, bringing us back to fellowship with our heavenly Father.

I was bound by what I was taught in church. I did not feel like God loved me; I was not worthy of Him to love me. Condemnation was taught.

God sent His Son to earth to show us what it was like to be a child of God. We are made in the image of our heavenly Father. (Genesis 1:27) says, "So God created man in His own image; in the image of God created He him; male and female created He them." He breathed life into us, and we became living souls. God is a spirit, and the breath we breathe is His spirit. His Word reads, "Fear not, only believe."

Our thinking separates us from God.

I did not believe I could live the way God wanted me to live.

I felt as if I was in prison, with bars across the windows, and with stockades that bound me hand and foot.

I have learned my mind is my greatest enemy. I continually struggled to be free. I kept reminding myself the greatest power known is within me, so I can break those fetters and be a free being.

I was programmed that I could not be as God wanted me to be. When I realized I was a child of God, I thought I had to do this and do that to get God to love me. Then by His mercy, the Word showed me that He paid the price. One time was enough. All was paid. All I had to do was believe I was His child; His spirit is in me, for I am made in His image.

My mind was what complicated the Gospel. God is simplicity and is easily entreated. He wants to become King of my life. He did not come in royal clothes and finery and did not issue laws and statues. He did not set up an earthy kingdom and did not rule the people.

He is the baby within us desiring to be made King and crown our minds with His love. His only law is love, and the only requirement is that we be at peace with Him as we believe.

I found God loves His people and does not want anyone to perish or be tormented. He wants us to have life and to live more abundantly.

He gives us life among the thorns and thistles and the challenges that we confront.

I needed to stop condemning myself, push on, and believe. God does not condemn me. He knows how I feel.

God's Son is shining upon this nation. He is leading His people out of bondage with His peace, love, and mercy as we go forth each day.

He is leading me amid the storms of life and gives me peace like a river without any envy, hatred, or strife. He gives me peace in the night and whispers I am His and He is mine!

As I seek His face, He is leading me to a land that flows with milk and honey. Me in Thee Thou in me, we two are one.

Stand in the truth, and tormenting minds shall be moved. Michael, God's archangel, is moving this day for us. Be lifted in your heart and mind, for He does bring peace, joy, love, and contentment.

4

Without Love, Life Is Empty

Without caring, all is gone.
For with love, we have the answer
Even though things go wrong.
Without love to lead and guide us,
There is no lamplight shining bright.
Trusting His love, as mercy surrounds us,
Will allow us to conquer fear and give us sight.

Without love, my life is ended.
No hope for me; my life is spent.
Without love, why keep on trying?
I am only kidding myself, and I am left crying.

Love, love, love, love.
Love will never fail me.
Love is the joy in sharing,
Love is the peace in caring.
Love: You cannot form it.
You cannot hold it or mold it,
Steal it or sell it.
For love cannot be bought.
You can win it only by giving.
Hold it only by living.
Know its joy by sharing.
Oh! To know love.
Only love will bring you peace.
Only love causes fear to cease.

Love will never fail.
Search for love.
You can surely feel His presence,
See the glow on the face that has it,
And see the doubts and fears go away
When there is love.
With love, there is liberty.
With love, there is wealth.
True love will free your brother.
Let him expand to worlds unknown.
Love, love, love, love,
Love will never fail me.
Love, love, love, love,
For in love is truth.

5

As We Think

We all know there is a lot of evil in this world. There has been from the beginning and will always be. But He has redeemed me with a price that no human can pay. It is free, it is given to me, and it cannot be taken back, but I can lose His peace by my thinking.

It is your thinking that can bring fear or peace of mind, because how you think makes a difference you will find.

His peace is our peace. He promised to lead and guide us into all truth. We need to go about our business and know that He will lead us into all truth.

There will always be wars and rumors of wars, and He will always be there to set us free.

We shall be set free, for His mercy holds. We are being set free now. Do you see what I see? You are being set free from the burden that has been upon all His people from the beginning of time.

Few have laid their thinking down long enough to listen to truth. Now as we are listening to the truth, He will set us free. All He asks is that we listen and let Him lead and guide us into all truth. Believe and trust, knowing that He cares. Remember that He will never leave us or forsake us.

As we pray without ceasing, we shall be safe from all harm that would befall us.

It seems right to worship as some worship, but do they know what they are worshipping? It has been handed down by humans until it does not even resemble the truth.

God does not want anyone left behind. All is well. Everyone is His child. Some are more obedient and seek Him more than others, but they are all His. He has redeemed everyone. Everyone was bought with a price. Jesus did it right the first time, and one time is enough.

We can go in peace, go in love, and go knowing that all is well. He loves everyone, even those who are unlovable. There are those who are unlovable. They know not His love. They are His children, but they were snatched away into destruction, and He wants them back so He can show them His love. For His love will win them back.

I have no doubt His love is enough. When we have a chance to do good, then we need to do good. He will be there to lead and guide us into all truth.

His spirit is our spirit when we listen to His voice. Do not fear to enter. Fear is the culprit. Faith and fear cannot dwell together in peace. We can go about our business and make our business God's business, but most of all, let peace reign in our hearts and minds.

For His mercy holds—wholly holds—for all to see. It makes you free from the shackles that keep you from being completely free.

He wants us to be in health and prosper, even as He prospers us. He wants us to prosper in all things, to prosper hand over hand, going about and healing the sick and doing away with pain, fear, doubt, and unbelief.

Fear of what others will think has kept great knowledge from being shared. Great scholars have been martyred for believing differently from what was acceptable in society. Many prophets were also martyred because people fear change.

People have their minds written so full of what is handed down through tradition that they have margin minds. Not much can be written on a margin. Sometimes there is just enough to cause confusion and fear of the unknown.

An open mind can only be written upon without fear. Fear comes first because it is unknown, a new idea. Try the fear. Did the new idea bring life to you, and could it bring life to others? If so, why fear?

The only concern we have—and it is a real concern—is the acceptance of those around us, who are afraid to believe anything new. We have many examples of that every day. We have had these examples through the ages. Jesus faced that. Changes have caused rebellions, wars, and so forth.

Somehow, through each battle a little of the new stays, and then later a little more is added. Keep the faith. God is patient and knows the beginning until the end.

6

Jesus Did Not Write a Book

He seeks those who will worship Him in their minds and deeds, in spirit and truth.

He did not write a book.

He did not have a church of His own to preach in.

He did not have a school to teach in.

Yet He was the greatest person who ever lived upon this earth.

More books have been written about Him.

More studies performed.

More recognition.

He performed more good deeds.

Healed more diseases.

Set more captives free and broke every yoke.

We are just a shadow of our heavenly Father.

He is all love and mercy, gentleness, kindness, and long-suffering.

As we become as little children and have not minds of our own, we will have complete trust in Him, knowing He will lead us to the right path.

7

John the Baptist Preached Repentance

Repent for letting unbelief rule and reign in your hearts and minds. Repent and receive God's gift of love. When we choose love, love then has the upper hand in our lives.

Then Peter said unto them, "Repent and be baptized every one of you in the name of Jesus Christ for the remission of your sins, and ye shall receive the gift of the Holy Ghost" (Acts 2:38). When God breathed His breath into us, we became living souls. Repent from not believing God dwells within. We are born by His spirit. Our spirits are made in His image. We are flesh, as we are made in our parents' images.

Jesus gave His life to take away our burden of unbelief that was present down through the ages since Adam and Eve, which is mentioned several times in this book. They believed not their Maker. Let doubt be washed away. Water is only a symbol of the spiritual meaning. There can be a comfort in a physical baptism.

If you take it spiritually, there is more to gain. Nothing changes until your spirit makes a change. Jesus was flesh as we are, and He listened to His Father. He did what His Father asked Him to do. He was completely submerged.

He said we would have to have the same baptism as He had, being completely submerged in His Father's trust. Remember that Jesus spoke in parables, and only the Spirit can interpret them so we can find life and truth in them.

We are to listen to the voice of our Father, which is the voice of love and comfort. We should not listen to the voice of fear and doubt—that would haunt our lives. For that voice is there too, and we must learn to distinguish between them. Sometimes we must cry out from within, "Show me the way."

A God of love never fails to show us the way if we wait. We must wait because fear and torment will rush us into more torment and fear. It breeds more of its kind.

We are wells of living water. Heaven is a place our spirits can abide in, up above the cares of this life.

Salvation is a way of life.

We are to live in peace when all unbelief is overcome. Until all is overcome, we will have seasons of peace and seasons of turmoil.

You can mix a little oil with water, and it does not really disturb the water; you can skim it off the top. The more oil you add, the harder it is to separate, and finally the water is more oil than water.

If we keep adding faith, where doubt was present, then unbelief is not seen anymore because God is peace. Do not forget that with our own minds, we cannot do this. Trying to do it will not work. We cannot clean up our lives.

We must let our spirits cry out for help. The spirit knows what makes for happiness. It knows what we need to go through to get there. The aim is to overcome evil with good so that we shall be like our elder brother, Jesus. We can be in complete harmony with the soul, mind, spirit, and body.

I used to think God was a way off somewhere, and He stood there ready to condemn me when I was not good. He does not condemn us. He lends a helping hand.

When we realize we have the greatest friend, we will know He is with us. Then peace can rule and reign in our mortal bodies.

We are the temple of God. He breathed into us the breath of life. He does not want anyone else sitting in our temple as King. He wants to be Lord and Master of our lives because only then can we have peace. That is what God wants: for His children to know peace.

Priests were an act of mercy from God until people realized that the altar is within us, so people confess their unbelief to God and ask forgiveness for not believing that God dwells within them. He came and gave His life to cleanse us from all that would keep us from believing we are God's children. When they realize God is within them, they can talk to their heavenly Father.

I can clearly see for the first time that in everything we do, we must answer to good and evil. There are only two forces, good and evil.

Know for sure that good will win.

God shows mercy to us when we are merciful to others. God is a God of an abundance of mercy. Because we are the temple of God's spirit, we are to portray His mercy.

God is alive. He is life. He has mercy on us until our minds can grasp that He wants to walk and talk with us. He is merciful when He sees we are afraid and cannot believe. God realizes we can be bound, restricted, and frightened. He knows we are trying to get good enough for His blessings. He is merciful until we receive the truth that all we must do is believe. He is our Father and cares for His children. He knows we cannot get good enough, so He is patient with us.

God is what we have need of, and all we need to do is ask in faith, believing that He is and that He is the rewarder of those who diligently seek Him.

When we find God, we will find ourselves. Then we do not rely on anyone else to keep us pumped up and encouraged, other than ourselves. When you know contentment, then and only then will you know your self-worth. You know where you came from, you know how you got to where you are today, and you know there is a way to get to where you want to go. You are satisfied with yourself, and you are truly blessed.

Sometimes compliments do not mean anything to us. We let them go over our heads. Sometimes we expect to be complimented, and that does not happen. Then we feel no one cares.

But when we know in whom we have believed, and we know that we are doing a good job and listening to His voice. Then and only then, do we not need praise from others. It really does not matter if we do not receive praise from the outside.

When we can supply our needs from within and feed ourselves with His Word, that is true contentment. That empty pit in our insides is filled. We are not looking to someone or something to satisfy us.

You will see I have used the quote "measure of faith" several times in this book. Romans 12:3 states, "For I say, through the grace given unto me, to every man that is among you, not to think of himself more highly than he ought to think, but to think soberly, according as God hath dealt every man the measure of faith." That measure of faith has grown to meet our needs and fulfill our desires. That is what we are all searching: to please, to be accepted, and to be needed and wanted.

We will become as one with our spirits, and then we no longer look outside of ourselves. We are enough.

That is what the phrase we hear so many times, "Learn to love yourself," means. Trust yourself to be all you need, spiritually and emotionally.

Fear is now gone; love is our motivation. Fear of not being accepted, fear of not being wanted, fear of failure—that is all gone. Those emotions are triggered from external things.

What we think of ourselves is what is important. We see ourselves as we really are. With all the faults and failures, we still have faith in knowing all things will work out.

This is new ground, and we will learn as we proceed.

One thing is for sure: the struggle will not be as bad as when we were looking for validation from without. That was an endless battle. Contentment and satisfaction can only be supplied from within.

When we love ourselves enough to listen to ourselves, then that voice of fear and doubt will stop playing in our heads. That recording will stop when we quit listening to it, stop believing it, and stop reacting to it.

Know that God never lets us down. Never! We simply need to listen for that still, small voice. That voice never condemns or finds fault. That voice leads and guides us to all truths.

8

We Are in Bondage, but Not Willingly

We are in bondage, but not willingly. Eve gave way to her mind. If Eve had believed that she was a child of God and that God was her Father, then they would not have been put out of the garden.

Moses''s people gave way to their minds and unbelief, and they could not enter the Promised Land. Jesus overcame His mind by the Word, which is spirit and life. Jesus shows us that we are children of God, even as He is.

But our minds keep us earthbound. When we realize our minds are our enemy, we seek to put down our minds to receive the mind of Christ. God's spirit and truth are greater, waiting at the door, ready to open the door when our minds are put down. Jesus's disciples understood some but did not understand it all. If you are still converting sinners (which is God's business) then you may be a scribe and Pharisee. You know not God's visitation to His people.

Jesus came and gave His life to take away the sin of unbelief.

What happens when people say they got saved? They believe in their hearts that Jesus loves them and that they are children of God.

We ask them to repent of all the sins they can think of, which are things that they have done that may not be right. They repent of things that do not even matter to God. Those things will take care of themselves when they know they have a loving Father who loves and cares for them and will never leave them or forsake them.

We put people down before we lift them up. Why?

That was not Jesus's plan. He came to give them life and to proclaim, "Come unto me, all ye that labor and are heavy laden, and I will give you rest" (Matthew 11:28).

People need to know what they are repenting of. They should repent for not believing that when they were born, the breath of life was breathed into them, and they became children of God, made in His image. They have spirits. The only repentance is that they have not believed that. That is the sin! My people perish due to a lack of knowledge. Jesus said unto the ruler of the synagogue, "Be not afraid, only believe (Mark 5:36). "Take my yoke upon you and learn of me; for I am meek and lowly in heart: and ye shall find rest unto your souls" (Matthew 11:29–30).

Jesus came and gave His life to redeem us back to our heavenly Father, to show us we are children of God even as He is.

This is what we have heard: telling us to do this and do that, and then we will be worthy. We are all unworthy for the price Jesus paid to redeem us back to God. Do not stop there. We are His children made in His image.

Their words are keeping us in bondage of fear, doubt, and unbelief.

I know few there be who find it, but Jesus still declared the truth. Fear not! Only believe!

The battle has always been good and evil, fear and trust, doubt and faith, our minds and God's mind, our spirits and God's Spirit.

The kingdom of God is completely different than any person can comprehend, without the wisdom of God. The temple of God is within us.

We were all condemned by the law. Jesus came and bought us back. His Spirit is as a small mustard seed, but it prevailed.

God let me know that if I would only believe, others would believe. Just because someone else does not share the truth I believe, that is no reason for me not to believe. He needs only one at a time to believe. Jesus redeemed humankind completely, with no reservations.

God breathed His life into each one of us, a body of flesh that we see, and a spirit in us that we do not see.

Just think of the burden lifted off people when they realize they are children of the King, born into the kingdom. (It is not "Do this, do not do that," trying to get good enough for God to love them.)

It is declared that you are a child of the King, made in God's image. No person has an attachment on you. Might and power will cease.

What about you must be born again? You are born into a world of fear and unbelief, which is sin. Then you find out you are the temple of a living God you are a child of the King. You are truly born again when you believe you are His child. All the fetters from your mind are cut loose.

"For all have sinned; and come short of the glory of God" (Romans 3:23). The sin is not believing He is in us, for we are made in His image.

What would happen if you start declaring on the street or to each person you meet, "You are a child of God"! You are a free human being. Drop that look of guilt and shame and condemnation. Go your way and believe you are a child of God. Go and sin no more. Stop that unbelief. Believe that God made you in His image! For God lives within you. Always remember you are God's child, and He wants the best for you. He paid the price and will give you a mind to be the best you can be.

The prodigal son forgot where his inheritance was. When he remembered, he returned. His father was waiting with open arms.

They have forgotten wherein His spirit lies.

That is what He meant when He told the people to go and sin no more. Stop the unbelief. I am with you, and I have always been with you. Just believe. Jesus paid the price once, and once was enough. He did not condemn the woman: "Neither do I condemn thee: go and sin no more" (John 8:11). He was saying to her that He was all she needed. It is a simple gospel, easily entreated.

It is fleshly thinking that keeps people in bondage.

What is fleshly thinking? Thinking with your fleshly mind and not your spirit. Your spirit is peace and joy in the Holy Ghost.

Mercy holds. How can I be in health and prosper? How can I?

I know that God's words are spirit, and they are life.

He has all power in heaven and on Earth.

There is none greater than He, none greater than His words, for they are spirit, and they are life.

9

My Prayer #1

Dear God, I am Your child, and I do not have to beg or plead when rejoicing or in need. You know what I have need of even before I ask. I do not know why You are waiting to deliver me, but I pray I am ready to receive the truth, because it is the truth that will set me free. You are right of course, and I thank You that You are always right. When we become mature, we put away childish things. We know without a shadow of a doubt that You love us and want only what is best, and You will not withhold anything good from Your children.

Dear Father, I ask for wisdom in knowing what to do. What is the truth?

Please give me a mind to believe and accomplish what the Spirit has sent to do. As Your Word reads, "My peace I give it to you, not as the world gives you peace, let not your heart be troubled: You believe in God, believe also in me. In my father's house are many mansions: if it were not so, I would have told you. I go to prepare a place for you. and if I go to prepare a place for you, I will come again, and receive you unto myself; and where I am, there ye may be also" (John 14:2–3). I know, God, that it cannot be the way the world thinks, or it would have failed many times. You have a better plan that will not let us down, one that is peace and joy in the Holy Spirit.

It is different from anything that we have ever thought or imagine. It must be entirely different.

Help us to receive it wholeheartedly. "Let not your heart be troubled neither let it be afraid." (John 14:27). When we love ourselves the way You love us You will then have control. Dear, God, I will do just that. I will not be troubled, and I will not be afraid. Give me a mind to know how to accomplish that. Thank You, Jesus. Amen.

10

God Within

We have within us a being not conceived by any earthly person. This is the spirit. Food and drink cannot nourish that spirit. When body and spirit become one, then we are as one flesh. It cannot become one unless both are nourished and come to maturity.

The flesh is not as important as the spirit, but the flesh must be nourished, or it will die and there will be no longer a dwelling place for the spirit. God is life, and He gives peace, rest, and comfort. We need to "watch ye, stand fast in the truth, quit like men, be strong" (1 Corinthians 16:13). We need to rest our minds. We believe that all was finished.

If He paid it all, no debt remains. Be strong in the Lord thy God. Be strong and like-minded. "And we know that all things work together for good to them that love God, to them who are called according to His purpose" (Romans 8:28).

We are a free people. He will lift the heavy burdens and let the oppressed go free. Drop the baggage and do not pick it back up. Let it drop and lie there. Let the oppressed go free.

Do not ever think it is not God's will. It is God's will because He made us, and He can repair us. He will repair us. If Jesus died—and He did, and arose again—then we can, and we will. Let the oppressed go free.

He is the Christ, the Son of the living God, who never sleeps nor slumbers. God does deliver. We shall enter that rest and receive the benefits. There are benefits, rests, peace, and comfort. We can know that all was finished. It is finished. It is the Sabbath day of the Lord. This is the day and time that the Lord hath made, and I will dwell therein. No worry, no hurry, when all is well.

Our lives can be different, and they will be complete. As I enter that rest, I will not be struggling within and without. It is finished; peace is here. Peace comes; it is finished.

When Jesus received the vinegar, he said, "It is finished: and he bowed His head and gave up the ghost" (John 19:30). It was finished, and all debts were paid. All repentance has ceased, and He endured it all; by His stripes we are healed.

If we speak God's words, they will not return void. Relax and know that He is all. He made us. He repairs us, and He redeems us back into fellowship with our holy Creator.

"This is the day which the Lord hath made; we will rejoice and be glad in it" (Psalm 118:24).

I believed that God is a good God. Then I began practicing that and would not let fear enter my mind. I would not let fear bind my mind. I would not let fear torment my mind. Fear had to go. I was deprogrammed and then reprogrammed. What do I do in other areas of my life? How can I break the binding from my mind?

By the spirit of truth that the world cannot receive, God breaks that binding. He comes to make a way where there is no way.

I do not know what is next unless God reveals it to me. The spirit dwells and lives in our mortal body—even the spirit of truth, which the world cannot know.

Jesus answered and said unto them, "Blessed art thou Simon Barjona for flesh and blood have not revealed it unto you, but my Father which is in heaven" (Matthew 16:17).

Our minds cannot figure it out. It must be revealed. As we open our minds to His revelations, we will be able to receive new life, new revelations, and new truths.

We do not put new wine into old bottles, lest they break. Our old traditions must be forsaken before new truths can be believed. There is not room for both.

Truth is new every day. There are new revelations each day, just as God provided food every day for the children Moses was bringing out of bondage. Our thinking binds our minds. We can have minds that are in Christ Jesus, that do not think it robbery to be equal to God. We can have minds to receive things that are of God.

Fruits of the spirit, which are love, peace, joy, long-suffering, kindness, and gentleness, show the Father. "He that hath an ear to hear, let him hear" (Matthew 11:15). Fear, doubt, and unbelief cannot receive the spirit of truth. As we listen to the still, small voice, we shall be led out.

God knows what is best for us and will reveal unto us truth that will set us free. It is all in His Word.

He will reveal unto us His will. His will is that you be in health and prosper. Simply believe.

We can talk to each other, give strength to one another, and give help to all who come to us. We will not turn away anyone, because we have help for each one. Our strength shall be enough because He is our strength. We know this and will depend upon Him.

Remember: He shall never leave you or forsake you.

Miracles can be in our hands to perform that which He has given us power to perform. It is not by might or by power, but by His Spirit that He shall heal the minds of our people.

Freedom is what we are after—freedom from our own minds. We have not thought for ourselves. We think as someone else has taught us to think. As we read His Word, we will listen to His teachings.

Many do not know where their source of supply comes from. As we listen to God's voice that is within, He will guide and direct our feet. "Therefore, whatsoever ye have spoken in darkness shall be heard in the light; and that which ye have spoken in the ear in closets shall be proclaimed upon the housetop" (Luke 12:3).

This a gospel worth telling. It is the gospel of peace.

Jesus sat down at the right hand of His Father until His enemies became His footstool. Jesus came in the Holy Spirit, the Spirit of truth (within each of us), and by His Word we are kept until our enemies become our footstool. Then God gives us His kingdom as He gave Jesus.

That takes me back to (St. John 16:26,) "At that day you shall ask in my name: and I say not unto you, that I will pray the

Father for you; for the Father himself loves you, because ye have loved me, and have believed that I am out from God." Face-to-face we speak as a Son to His Father, and the Father knows what we have need of and speaks back.

Jesus is the King of kings, and we crown Him Lord of lords. Jesus keeps us until we are fully redeemed, and our souls are brought back to a perfect spirit. We speak face-to-face, a constant flow. The windows of heaven are opened. Jesus was a ransom paid for our souls.

Jesus is the spirit of God, and He showed us we are part of that spirit, and that spirit is in us. When we were born, the breath of life was breathed into us. Jesus is the door into the sheepfold.

Jesus is the mediator until we reach a perfect spirit, by trusting that God completely is within us.

We are joint heirs with Christ. When we have a perfect spirit, then we speak face-to-face with God the Father. His word is His body, our bodies.

Persecution shall arise, but we are not to be dismayed. Many shall come and many shall go, but God will help us stand firm. For we shall know the truth, and the truth shall set us free. He will hold us in all things. God comes to lead us out of bondage, out of ourselves into the glorious freedom He has prepared for us: a place of rest. No more striving, contention, warring against ourselves, or defeating our own purpose.

You strive not against flesh and blood, but powers and principalities and wickedness in high places. Perfection of spirit, mind, and body is the goal.

As we learn to love our neighbors as ourselves, we will reap the rewards of spiritual wealth. Peace and joy await us as we kneel at the cross and answer the call. Peace and joy shall be ours throughout all eternity because God has loved us and called us.

11

God Is Love

God is love, joy, and peace.
God is love and everything you need.
Though you cannot grasp His hand,
God is in the land.
God is love, and love is grand.
Peace and joy at His command.
God is love on land and sea.
My God is love; just believe.
Love is real; hold it dearly.
Love is real; know sincerely.
His love is free when you come unto Him.
Bring your doubts and fears,
Bring your heartfelt tears.
Open wide your mind,
Know the joy of love sublime.
Love is real.
Holy peace He gives to you.
His Holy peace will see you through.
The lonely hours of the day,
The believing hours when you pray.
His peace He freely gives to you.
Holy love and peace are true.
For He has given life to you.
Wait, for peace.

12

Peace with Your Fellow Man

When I am at peace with myself; I am at peace with others. When we lift Jesus, He can draw all people unto Him. He does the drawing. It is the goodness of God that draws all people to Him.

He shows mercy to one and all. He has given us something worth living for. It is His people. It is something more than wealth or fame. His people are worth living for.

He wants His people to see they are spiritual beings. They are called out and will not be denied His fellowship. His people are a free people.

Free.

He is bringing us out of bondage. He paid the price so we can have peace, rest, and comfort. Above all things, He wants you to be at peace with yourself.

His people are in bondage to their own thinking. As they think, so they do. Yes, I see a way. Mercy is coming. I see love and mercy coming, and minds are moving for us this day.

The archangel Michael will move minds for us today. Love will lift your mind wholly and acceptable unto God. For love lifts the minds. I see love lifting the mind completely. Mercy is coming to give strength, courage, and open our minds. We shall be healed.

As we go about sharing God's love; they will say surely God is in this place. Because God lives, those hungry hearts shall be fed. Those hungry eyes shall see peace, everlasting rest, and security.

God's words shall awaken them out of their sleep. Yes, they are asleep, but as God gently awakens them out of their sleep, they shall receive peace and rest.

Contentment, peace, and rest shall be ours to have. To be able to give is a wonderful, satisfying feeling, a lifting, light, airy feeling.

This is meat to eat that you know not of. Many needs shall be met sooner than you think.

13

Nothing Have I Seen

Nothing have I seen,
While here I live,
To bring peace of mind,
Or life would give.
Nothing satisfied,
Nothing lasted,
Nothing was perfect, always a blemish.

Oh! For a moment, many times I thought
I had found what I had sought.
Only to be let down, torn, and wrought.
It was not here, what He had bought.
It was not here; where else could I look?
It was then God began to open His precious book.
A Book of Life, treasures unknown.
Filled with jewels, among the gold was sown.
This must be true for this burned inside.
It began to lighten my load and give me sight.
Higher He caused me to look each day,
Higher than where I had looked always.

Jesus came that we might have life.
Jesus came among the strife.
His Father kept Him until His day.
Why? He said He would keep me
I had only to pray and believe.
That He loved me, the price was paid.

Come with me, come today.
Take a drink from the fountain of life.
Look in the Book, search for life.
You will not search long until you will see
There is one who cares and comforts thee.
Oh! The joy of one who will share.
Oh! There is joy without despair.
Remember, keep looking up
Then we will not sink.
Reach out your hand,
And with His hand link.

14

Mystery

We are truly a mystery, even to ourselves.

We think we know what we need when we attain it, there is sometimes a void. If only we could have the mind of an eighty-five-year-old when we are twenty years of age. Oh! The glory we could witness in our lifetime. The pitfalls we would miss. The joys we would take time to share.

Rushing would slow, caring would increase, giving would be utmost. We would be able to see how short life really is.

Pride robs us so many times from life's greatest moments. If we would only put standards on ourselves, learn to accept others as they are, then hate and resentment would die.

We are our brother's keeper. We are to show love and not rob others of that experience.

I have learned Jesus needs to be loved, revered, nourished, and guarded until He is King of our lives.

Oh! The peace in knowing we do not have to get good enough to please God. Do not do this and do that. Simply listen to the still, small voice that is leading and guiding.

Just as sure as we speak, God can speak. He is our Father and dwells within. Then answered Jesus and said unto them, "Verily,

verily I say unto you, The Son can do nothing of himself, but what he sees the Father do: for what things soever he doeth, these also doeth the Son likewise" (John 5:19).

All things are going to be shaken. This earth is going to quake. There will be wars and rumors of wars, but the truth will prevail. God is a messenger of peace. When all the chaff is sifted, we have peace, contentment, mercy, and love.

We all have problems, and we all suffer many times. The difference is if we keep hope, we will be successful and come out on the other side of our problems. I know we can find answers that deliver.

I have learned you cannot change someone else. That person must want to change first. If people want to be led out, you can shine some light on their pathway. You can let them know you trod the same path, that there is light at the end of the tunnel.

The reason we are miserable is that we are going against what is best for us, and we know that. We are miserable and striving against what is best for us. We are at war with ourselves. Who is going to win?

When the enemy is cast down from sitting on the throne in our thinking, the war will be over. We have what is good for us at our taking or refusing. We are sick and tired of sharing the throne.

Why do we struggle so? Why is the struggle even there? God's spirit is in a fleshly body. We have God's spirit within us, and we have our earthly spirit within us.

That was the cross that Jesus faced for us. He conquered death, torment, and the grave. He was our example. He did not say it would be easy to conquer our minds, but He did say be yoked with Him, for His yoke is easy and His burden light.

Again, we are double minded. We too must become one flesh. Love is greater than hate. We can entertain love for ourselves, or contempt for ourselves. Our thinking puts to death God's thinking, so we are in torment, and then we are in the grave or held in bondage to our thinking because it is not the right thinking, because it wars against what is best for us.

As I just wrote, He conquered death, torment, and the grave. He conquered that. Oh! Maybe He conquered that? No! He did conquer that. So, we know we can too!

We are thankful the truth was found to set us free.

15

Find Your Place with God Today

Find your place with God today.
Whether large or small, do not be dismayed.
God will equip you with grace, you will see,
To perform that task, whatever it may be.

His perfect will is not for us to comprehend.
That is why we must on Him wholly depend.
We are not enough to make the right choice.
When depending on Him, our souls do rejoice.

All things work together for good.
Though grievous for a season they may seem.
Patience will win out
If we hold on and believe.
Do not limit God's power; He can supply our need.
Why fret about material things?
He will provide enough, and more indeed.

Thank You, Jesus, for breath today
To whisper, "I love You," from these lips of clay.
The sweetest peace sweeps over my soul
When I whisper, "I love You, it's You I adore."

16

We Talk of Love

We talk of love to everyone, but about love for ourselves, we judge ourselves too harshly. We do not give ourselves the benefit of the doubt. We are merciless to our own selves.

We hamper.
We bind.
We cripple.
We hold down.
We hold back.
We keep hidden.
We are not our own best friend.

We do not like ourselves. We hate instead of waiting. Do you fit the picture of the person whom we have mutilated?

We would never think of treating someone else as badly as we treat ourselves. Sometimes we kill our own spirits by not listening to ourselves. We are our own worst enemies.

If we start being kind and merciful to someone who has always been beat done, what happens? We see that person blossom and bloom and reach out and grow and have confidence.

We need to climb every mountain until we find our dream. Give comfort and understanding to ourselves. Give ourselves the benefit of the doubt.

Try to see your side. Understand yourself. Take up for yourself. Be your own best friend. Go overboard to be good to you. Give yourself love—real love.

Love does not change under any circumstances. Never beat yourself down—never. There is a reason for all things. Listen to yourself. Listen to your ideas. Listen to your talk. Listen to your reasoning. Do not nag yourself. Be your own best friend. Listen to your dreams. Listen to your complaints. Listen to your disappointments.

I have only one audible life to live. May I give to you what I have found to be life to me. You may evaluate my experiences; they may be stepping-stones to your finding happiness.

I only want for you what I desire for myself. Life everlasting, peace and contentment, joy, and love.

The place I found life was in myself. If I could forgive myself for not believing I am a child of God, then I am forgiven. Jesus forgave me with His blood. "Whatsoever thou shalt loose on earth, shall be loosed in heaven" (Matthew 16:19 KJV).

Maybe we have let someone else beat us down. It is time to take control. I have found out God loves His children. He comes to make a way where there is no way. He makes a way in the desert and in the valley of defeat. He fights our battles for us. He changes people's minds that we thought could never be changed. God sees a way being made.

Look up and see the silver lining. There is hope, so never doubt. Faith will win out.

17

God Speaks Peace to Us: Fear Not

Fear not! You have heard Me say before.
Fear not, only believe!
Please believe I do not fail.
Fear not. and peace shall prevail.
Love and mercy are yours.
Peace and contentment.
You have paid the price.
The price of letting Me be your friend and guide.
There is peace in the raging waters.
There is peace amid torment.
There is peace. for I made all things well.
Support from My loving arms you shall always have.
Support and gentleness and warmth, tenderness and caring.
You deserve the best; you have stood the test.

18

Pride

We need to watch out for pride. It always comes before a fall. But confidence is strength. Be not weary in well doing; you shall surely receive the profits. What you give shall return to you.

God has given us strength for every challenge we shall meet. He has given us power to face life. We have the necessary tools. You may not be aware of the strength that you have. You have a powerful resource that has never been tapped into.

Rest again. I say rest, for the evils of this day are enough. Tomorrow is another day. God will be with you tomorrow, even as He is with you today.

Give that which He has given unto you. It shall be food for another. Rest and contentment shall be yours when His life flows through unto others. Grace and truth can be compared to a rose in full bloom at its peak of beauty, breathtaking and glorious.

Rest again, God says rest. You shall find rest, even as He speaks to you this day. You shall find rest. There shall be a peace flowing over you, and you shall find rest, peace, and comfort.

Love yourself like God loves you. Torment shall you drive out. Fear shall have to leave. Be good to yourself. Then you shall know how to free others.

Struggles, struggles unending.

You cannot see the end of struggles.

Stop! Without challenges, you would never know your strength. We are a mighty people and a strong nation. We can rise above our fears and face our struggles with courage and fortitude.

God did not promise you a bed of roses. But He did promise you strength to meet every need, courage to open every door, and faith to meet each challenge.

Are you weary today? Take it easy. God wants you to be good to yourself. He does not want any harm to befall you, for you are a pearl of great price.

I see the cloak of fear that keeps God's light from shining through to free your mind. Be not dismayed; His light shall break through every barrier that is raised against you. God's peace is your peace. God's understanding is your understanding.

When you see yourself as you really are? Then shall you see God. Life is yours this day, free and clear.

Sometimes the load seems greater than we can bear. Hold on! Just one more mile. We will find a way.

Rushing waters, thunder, and lightning are crashing and beating upon your life. Be still and know there is a way; you have only to seek to find it.

19

God Comforts Us

"Do not tune Me out; I am your friend. I am on your side. I will fight for you and will be there to comfort and see you through. I will not withhold any good thing from you. I want for you the best. Wishful thinking should never take the place of getting the job accomplished.

"Chart your course, and follow with all might? Be at peace with yourself. Believe that I dwell within to lead and guide you.

"I have given each one of you a talent. As you use that talent, you can push through your fears. Erase those doubts. Dare to step out because each challenge can be a rewarding adventure."

Mountains, mountains. I see those mountains.

Insurmountable, you say?

We can take that mountain apart piece by piece, and we will see that mountain disappear before our eyes. You can do whatever you desire to do. Only believe that all things are possible. I see those mountains moving. Yes, they are moving out of our way this day.

Mercy is coming our way. Remember that He is the God of mercy.

To free your soul from a lifetime of fear sometimes takes a lifetime. It is a freedom never known to us. Love is yours this day; with peace and understanding, condemnation shall vanish, and guilt shall have to flee.

I know God's love shall overshadow all evil that looms so great and that would drown us. God's love is greater.

God has wisdom for us in every situation. Simply reach out and ask for it, and you will have what you ask for. Wisdom is yours. Take it, please.

It is your heritage. How can you fail with God on your side?

He is our friend. He fails not. What looks like failures are only stepping-stones to something better. Pick up the pieces and put them back together. Look for life, and you shall find it.

21

Our Spirit Speaks

My ways are love and mercy:
Not torment, fear nor condemnation, guilt nor dread.
I am tenderness, gentleness, and confidence.
I see you, and I believe in you.
I know what you are made of.
I know you can accomplish what you desire.
I have faith in you, for I dwell within.
Listen to My voice and know that I am your God.
I speak peace during the raging storms.
I speak comfort amid travail.
You were born with a measure of faith.
Let that seed mature in you.
Let it nourish and blossom and come forth to full stature.
I am life.
I am peace.
I am understanding.
I am whatever you have need of.
I want what is best for you.
Stop condemning yourself.
I do not condemn you.
I know how you feel, and I understand you.
Mercy shall be with you wherever you go.
Mercy shall hold you and hold you close.

Peace shall calm the waters.
Peace shall answer your needs.
Peace shall be within you, you will find.
I give perfect peace to those that endure.

21

Choose Faith

God wills that we choose faith and trust.

Both are set before us. We can be yoked with the stronger one, and the good within us will win out. We will be determined until that mind of distrust is brought into subjection.

His yoke is easy, and His burden is light.

He takes care of the lilies of the field. He sees the sparrow that falls. He hears us when we cry, and He speaks peace to our hearts, minds, and spirits. For He has been with us from the beginning.

We all have an inheritance. We can go into a far country and waste all that we have, even as the prodigal son. You notice he was still his son, a beloved son, even though he wasted all that his father had given him. He was just as much of a son as the one who stayed, obeyed his father's wishes, and rested in his father's wealth. He was not any less of a son because he ran away.

The son paid a dear price for running and not believing his father. He did not believe that the best place to be was in his father's house.

It is the same reason Eve partook of the fruit in the garden: she did not believe her Father knew best. Eve is the type of spirit taken out of self, coming from the fleshly mind. It pulls against the things that are best for us. It will pull, tear, rip, and destroy.

We did not put ourselves in this place, so do not feel like a failure when you find yourself in bondage.

Our repentance is that we did not believe that God is in us. We do not follow His voice of trust but let fear lead us. The spirit of God within us is to lead and guide, to make a way where there is no way.

His spirit does not hamper our lives but shapes and molds us to glorify him. It works only for our good.

He made us His children.

That is bringing glory to our Father: letting Him be glorified in our lives. God sent His Son to show us His inheritance. Jesus's inheritance did not fail Him. He was victorious over death, torment, and the grave.

We can believe that God's spirit will arise up and become Lord of our lives. Victorious! He wrestled until His sweat became as droplets of blood, but He was victorious. Who will hold on when all odds are against us? Our spirits will hold! We are yoked with the greater power.

We are on the winning side; we can fulfill our potential in life. Do not draw back.

If we want to do something, we simply need to go do it. We deserve to do it, so do not draw back.

Feel free to do it. Do not feel unworthy. Do what fulfills your life now. Climb every mountain and forge every stream until you find your dream.

Leave no stone unturned. Shake those fears, doubts, and unbelief. They will not stand! Go ahead and shake them! Press through—feel free! Encourage others to find their dreams.

Peace is yours this day. God has given us peace. Make those dreams realities. Create and blossom forth. What is life, but what you make of it?

We were not afraid people would make fun of what we believed, so do not be afraid that people will make fun of what you do or say.

God's people need help. You are the one to help them because you want to, not because you felt pressured to do it. Because love does not pressure. Love lets you do as you see fit. Love never pressures. So do not pressure yourself, ever! Help others because you see the need. Let up on the pressure!

My people are miserable. They are unhappy, very unhappy. Too many pressures, too many condemnations, too many fears of failure. They are Afraid to try what they feel in their gut. Instead, they should dare to believe that all things are possible to those who believe.

Go ahead, shake that ship of doubt. You can swim to shore. You have the talents—pursue them! Multiply them because they are gifts. Use them for your good and others' good. Promote God's cause because it is your cause. Pursue happiness and give of yourself to others to find happiness for yourself. Satisfaction is in seeing others happy. Happiness will be your reward. Others will be happy because of you.

We can give to them. Give to them life more abundantly. That is where your happiness lies.

Everyone has a song to sing. It was with us from the beginning. We simply need to give it voice so it can ring loud and clear, directing us through the darkness and into the everlasting light of day.

Onward to truth through tunnels and over mountains. Upward to victory, coaxing, nudging, and willing to wait, until the signals are manifest. Striving with the inner turmoil, going against what may seem right to those around us. Knowing we must step to the beat of our own heart. Being willing to lay aside our fears to receive new thinking that will bring peace to our lives.

Love is the only way. Love yourself because you are the temple of God. I do not know a God other than a God of love. It is the goodness of God that has brought me to repent, of not believing that He lives within.

There is a way that seems to be right, and then there is a way that is right. What do we tell God's people? That all things are possible to those who believe. He can lead and guide them into truth without outside help.

Has He not led us all the way, step by step each day? The song by John W. Peterson, "Jesus Led Me All the Way," states, "I will tell the saints and angels when I lay my burdens down; Jesus, Jesus, led me all the way."

We can tell people to seek God. Seek Him until an answer comes, for the answer will come. Do not give up, for the answer will come in due time.

Seek His face until you see Him high and lifted, above every tongue or pen. Be lifted with Him. He is the way, the truth, and the life. He will lead and guide His people into all truth.

They need not that people should teach them; He will be their God, and they shall be His people.

"Behold, the Lord's hand is not shortened, that it cannot save; neither His ear heavy that He cannot hear" (Isaiah 59:1). He is what we have need of today, if only we believe.

Do not be afraid to listen to His voice; He will not steer you wrong. Try the spirits to see if they are of God. Are they against Him being within? Are they against love being your motivator, instead of fear? Do they bring frustration, doubts, and torments?

His voice will lift our spirits. "I am the way, the truth, and the life: no man cometh to the Father, but by me" (John 14:6).

First believe that He is, and that He is the rewarder of those who diligently seek Him. He will never leave you or forsake you. He will be with you until the end. He knew the end from the beginning.

I know when you see no way, then He sees a way, whether in the desert, in the floods, and during the famines.

He is a way maker, and nothing happens to you unless He knows about it. We learn obedience by the things which we suffer.

Churches were built on someone's knowledge of seeking God, and they should be for one main reason: seeking to know more about the Lord within. Each one of us is different, so what works for you may not be my answer. I must seek God for myself. We were all reared differently.

We fear to listen to our Father's voice. We doubt that it is His voice when we hear it. We do not believe; we push it aside, and then torment reigns instead of peace. His sheep know His voice. He is a gentleman; He will never push or make you believe, and He will never condemn you for not believing. He will bring the truth back to our remembrance, until it is life unto us.

He is faithful.

He does not start something and stop off in the middle. He knows where He is leading us, knows how to do it, and is successful. He is leading us into complete trust in Him. He is not leading us into a doctrine but, a way of life. Little by little, the mustard seed grows until it develops into His love. He does not know failure.

It is no wonder Jesus drove the money changers out of the synagogue. They were padding their pockets and selling peace. Our minds have enmity against God.

We need to emphasize the deliverer. What did Daniel do? He obeyed God rather than any person; he listened to the still, small voice. What did the three Hebrew children do? They obeyed God rather than anyone; they listened to His voice.

What did Abraham do? He listened to the voice of God.

Jesus did nothing save what His Father told him to do. He came to glorify His Father. He could do nothing by Himself. "Trust and obey" are His words. Obedience is better than sacrifice.

Everyone needs to know when you seek Him, you will find Him. At your darkest hour, keep holding on and believing. You know there is a way that seems right, and then there is a way that is right. He comes to show His people the way that is right.

He will be high and lifted. He shall go forth and conquer. He will not be denied. He will not lose one that the Father has given Him.

He does not give His people a spirit to go back into perdition.

He does not give His people a spirit of fear. He comforts His people. He does not condemn. He understands and feels what they feel.

We cannot, by ourselves, help ourselves. He is the way maker; His route is love. His love shall overpower His people. They shall be flabbergasted by His love.

In the hour that you seek Him, you will find Him. You need not read how-to books. Your experience is the best teacher, following His directions. Be taught by the Master Himself.

There are no substitute teachers. The teacher is within you. Search the scriptures, for in them you think you have eternal life.

God does not leave His work to His inferior officers because God does not slumber or sleep. He is always on the job—never late, always on time. He delivers, and He does not shirk. Ask, and you shall receive. Knock, and it shall be opened unto you. Seek, and ye shall find.

Ask in faith believing, and you shall receive. Torment cannot prevail against my God.

We are not recommending a has-been. He is. And He is a rewarder of those who diligently seek Him. We will find Him when we seek Him with all our hearts.

Step by step, here a little and there a little. Prayer by prayer, hope by hope, faith by faith. Never yielding until the answer comes. We are in bondage; we travail until the light comes forth. We are blinded—the God of this world has blinded our eyes.

God will continue to show us the way as we seek His face daily, without ceasing.

> Jesus saith unto him, "I am the way, the truth, and the life: no man cometh unto the Father, but by me." (John 14:6)

> These things have I written unto you concerning them that seduce you, but the anointing which ye have received abides in you, and ye need not that any man teach you: but as the same anointing teaches you of all things, and is truth, and is no lie, and even as it hath taught you, ye shall abide in Him. (1 John 2:27)

He is our teacher; seek Him early, and you shall find Him early. He is love. It is His goodness that leads His people to repent of not believing. Love is the fulfillment of the law. Love drives out fear. Love cushions our every fall.

No person should be lifted. No church should be lifted. No congregation should be lifted. No gift should be lifted. No doctrine should be lifted.

Only Jesus is the breath of life within each one of us. The very breath that we breathe is God. We are all creatures of God. We are not all obedient children, but we are made in the image of God.

"If I be lifted up from the earth, I will draw all men unto me" (John 12:32).

Tongues are not the answer. Fasting is not the answer. Gifts are not the answer. The law is not the answer. Denomination is not the answer. Church is not the answer. Tithing is not the answer.

Seeking peace until we find it is the answer, the utmost goal. Not that these things may be bad.

Listen to the still, small voice. Seek, and ye shall find. Knock, and it shall be opened unto you. Ask God to show you like He really is. Seek until God is revealed unto you, until you realize He is the door. Knock until He is real in your life.

He will open the door that no one can open. You will find that He is love beyond any imagination.

He is never condemning. He is always leading to show us the way. No one has the franchise on God. He is free to one and all. He is the God of Abraham, Isaac, and Jacob. And He is our God.

He will not have any other gods before Him. You will not find peace if you have other gods before Him. He is the way maker. "All that the Father giveth me shall come to me; and him that cometh to me I will in no wise cast out" (John 6:37). "I am Alpha and Omega, the beginning and the end, the first and the last" (Revelation 22:13).

He changes not. His words are spirit, and they are life. You do not have to reach up to pull Him down or reach down and pull Him up. He is in us, even in our mouths. Remember the words He speaks because they are spirit and life.

22

The Word Is an Anchor

I love my people; I bring them in.
I love my people out of their sins,
Of fear and doubt and unbelief.
I give rest if they will only receive.

Why struggle within and without? With fears,
torment, disappointment, and doubt?
Blind and maimed, our minds cannot see
There's hope if there is life. Take it, please.
The Word of God is the anchor sure,
One that is secured with a love that is pure.
Everything else has been tried and failed.
The Word of God has always prevailed.
The Word is nigh you, even in your mouth.
God has made us vessels, His truth to tell.
Be a useful vessel, filled to the brim,
So, a thirsty soul can be refreshed by Him.

You can harbor fears and doubts,
Or you can lay them aside and come on out.
Perfect love will cast out fear.
Find it today; hold it dear.
We have a savior, the King of the Jews.
His words are final, and respect due.
The King wants to live and reign in the heart
To give peace and rest, and His love impart.

He asks only that we love by word and deed.
That is not asking too much for all that we will receive.
The secret of life is giving of ourselves,
If only a hello, handshake, or nod.
It is a seed of love, sent forth from God.

23

His Life-Giving Words:

To know Me
Is to love Me,
For I am love.
I am what you have need of this day.
Do not draw back from finding out who I really am.
You can trust Me to the fullest.
Remember, I am nothing like what you have been taught.
I work for you.
I search out the hidden meanings; I bring all things to light.
I look beyond and underneath.
I bring calmness, not frustration.
Fear will keep you from finding Me in my fullness.
Did I not create your mind?
Can I not take care of it?
Those who draw back will never know the
freedom I have prepared for them.
For those who seek Me will find me in all my glory.
Thank You, Father.

24

Believe All Things Are Possible

As we believe all things are possible, God's words will not die. I was born, bound hand and foot, and mind and soul were in bondage. Afraid to turn any direction. Afraid to move spiritually.

I did not think very highly of myself. I did not think I was as good as other people. I was afraid to declare what I believed. I was in the chains of fear.

Gradually, I believed my way out. The portion of faith, born inside of me, kept me plugging on until little by little, my faith was completely released. Fear was gone, never to return, buried in the sea of forgetfulness, never to be remembered or to do any harm.

Opposition shall arise, so be not dismayed. We shall survive with dignity and honor. Truth shall be our guide. Believe me, God shall never fail us or let us go uncared for. He shall always befriend us.

Truth is ours this day.

Truth shall be declared among many nations, and many shall cry out, "Truly this is of God."

A miracle working, Lord of all.

And He shall not fail His people who depend upon Him.

25

Talking to God

Dear God, I know the church of today will not like the way You deliver Your people, because it is by the spirit.

Dear God, I see the church world seeking You under the law. There is condemnation of might and power. All we need to do is believe that You dwell within each one of us. You breathed life into each one of us.

You will lead us and guide us into all truth.

We are trying to become good enough for You to dwell within, but You were there all the time.

There must be a strategy to use that will not offend our brothers and sisters.

There must be a course chartered that will work. The only way is love and mercy. Showing mercy on how they believe but loving them enough to point out another way.

I see the way being clear for You to lead Your people out of bondage. I see a way being made for You to lead them out of the way that they have charted their course. Fear has caused Your people to be bound hand and foot. They know not that You are love and mercy and long-suffering and gentleness and kindness. They think that You are demanding. But You are their friend who will never fail them or condemn them.

They can lean on You. They can trust You. They can draw upon Your resources. You can be trusted to give them wisdom and understanding. You will lead them and guide them.

You shall never leave them nor for sake them. You shall always be with them until the end of the Earth. They shall never be alone. You are their God, and they are Your people. Long have You sought for a people whose God is the Lord.

Long have You suffered to find a people who would believe You, not doubt Your existence, and not betray You. Long have You searched for someone to lead Your people out of bondage.

Long, long have You waited to buy us with a price that shall not fail us in due season.

Your people shall know Your existence. They shall prosper in the knowledge that You are a living God who lives in them.

You may be a baby in some, a toddler in others, children in others, and men in some. You shall raise some up to lead your people out of bondage.

A people will stand straight and tall and not waver, knowing that You shall not fail Your people. This is a people whose God is the Lord.

We are all Your children, but some have not followed the way of their Father. They have followed other gods, and therefore they are in torment here on Earth. If we are breathing, You, breathed into us that breath of life.

What we do with this life can bring honor and glory, or destruction with dishonor and torment. How did Jesus, Your Son, benefit by You?

He set at liberty those minds that would bind Him and keep Him from being a whole person.

He loosened those oppressed feelings within Himself. He healed the brokenhearted when others let Him down. He felt everything we felt.

He was free, set free! Thank You, Father.

26

A Living Spirit

Fear in food and drink.

Why are we tormented over this? We need to read the Bible.

For we would find that is not what goes into the body that defiles us.

But what issues out evil works when they get to the root of evil works?

What do we find? You guessed it: Fear. Fear is the culprit.

We fear to let ourselves believe that God is in us.

Fear of failure and acceptance, so the outcome is envy, strife, murder, and hate.

When we learn to replace fear with love and trust, then what comes out of us will not be defiled.

The wrong food and drink are not transgressions against our souls but against our bodies.

The apostle Paul says he could do all things, and it would not harm his spirit.

He also says it was not profitable for his body. He knew that if he wanted to live, he had to take good care of his body.

As we learn to be good to our spirits, we will learn to be kind to these bodies. Be at peace with yourself. Know that He lives within to lead and to guide.

The chains of fear are real only if we allow them to be.

Meet your person. In so doing shall you meet God! Face-to-face shall you meet your Maker. You are what you allow yourself to be.

You can change, you can free yourself. You can arise from the dead and receive life. Or you can remain in the grave, bound hand, and foot. The chains of fear are real.

But only if we allow them to be. Only if we allow darkness to overshadow. For when they are uncovered and brought to light, darkness is no longer present.

Do you dare to be different, standing alone? Yet you are bound to your neighbor, being true to yourself, without convincing another of your strength, living and let live.

Waiting on the sideline until help is needed.

Not pushing or shoving, just being there.

Who cares enough to search to free themselves? Who cares enough to search to free their neighbors? Burning the candle until the wee hours in the laboratory of life, mixing the vials of wisdom until the right mixture is found.

Testing and trying, time after time. Knowing the results will be the formula for life.

We are undernourished. Our bodies are overfed, but our spirits are starved, bordering on starvation. There is a famine in the land—not for earthly food but for the spirit. It hungers for the Word that proceeds from the mouth of God.

With our words, we either bless or condemn.

We should deny ourselves, take up our cross, and follow our spirit. What was the cross that Jesus bore? His life was the cross. He carried a cross because of the life that He lived. He believed His Father. He would have never had a cross to bear if Adam and Eve had believed their Father.

The life we live is a cross. He hangs between two crosses: One pulled against him, our earthly bodies. One pulled with Him, our spiritual bodies. He was in the middle. We are suspended between two desires, two crosses.

We are in between, one pulling against, one relinquishing to do God's will. One for, one against. Our spirits, God's spirit. We are spirit. We are spirits put into these earthly bodies.

We are living souls. We have a choice.

We have an opportunity to live and let live. We are spirit. Only the spirit listens to the voice of God.

Only a spirit knows the spirit of God. Only our spirit knows our spirit. When we surrender our spirit to God's spirit, then we have faith in our Lord and Savior, the spirit of God that dwells within us. We have the mind of Christ. We do not listen to it.

Our voices are louder, more demanding. It is not in the thunder or lightning, but in the still, small voice.

Our conscious, our spirit, our soul, our mind listens as we let that same mind be in us. Jesus thought it not robbery to be equal with God. He thought it not robbery to think as He thought. He thought it not robbery to do what God desired for His life.

God made us a living spirit. A spirit is not flesh and bone. The spirit dwells in the body made with flesh and bone. Our life is in our spirit. We had the breath of life breathed into us when we were born. We became a body and a spirit.

The body is dead without the spirit dwelling within. When we die, the breath is gone. Our spirit is gone out of us. Our life goes out. Therefore, we cannot live without the spirit.

To keep this body alive, to have a body for the spirit to dwell within, we need to be healthy. Because we did not make this body or make the spirit, neither has anything to do with having the spirit dwell within.

We need to rely upon our spirit to know what is best for us. We do what kept our elderly brother alive. Jesus prayed the Lord's Prayer. He taught us to do that too. Jesus suffered as we do. He was flesh, with His spirit dwelling within. He overcame the difficulties of living in the flesh, even as we can do.

> Great is thy faithfulness, morning by morning new mercies I see. All I have needed, thy hands have provided, Great is thy faithfulness, Oh! Lord to me.

> —Thomas Chisholm, "Great Is Thy Faithfulness"

"The Lord is my shepherd; I shall not want" (Psalm 23:1).

"Our father which art in heaven Hallowed be thy name. Thy Kingdom come Thy will be done in earth, as it is in heaven. Give us this day Our daily bread. Forgive us our debts as we forgive our debtors. And lead us not into temptation but deliver us from evil: For thine is the kingdom, the power, and the glory, forever, Amen" (Matthew 6:9–13).

For the kingdom is the Lord's.

We pray His will be done upon this earth and in our bodies, where His kingdom dwells. He has all power as He directs our footsteps. He knows what we have need of even before we ask. It is easy to be yoked with God. We are not in this alone. The power is in God. Being yoked to Him in spirit and truth, I pray, "Dear God, I am Yours. No part of me is mine. I give You my all. In Your hands I resign."

To be at peace, we have only to rely upon God to lead us and guide us into all truth. And we must believe He will not lead us into temptation, but with the temptation He will make a way for our escape. This kingdom within us is not ours. It was not put there by us; it will not stay there by us.

It will not go away by us. Why do we think we can control this kingdom? Nothing about it was made by humans.

How can we understand how to command something that we had nothing to do with putting it there? The battle is the Lord's.

We are learning to break our thinking and break our self-control. We cannot do it alone.

His yoke is easy, and His burden is light.

I feel like going outside and yelling at the top of my voice. I have found the way, the truth, and the life. We have only to come unto God, the author and finisher of our faith.

Why do we take over in the middle? Why do we think we have control over something that is all spirit? If I want to be healthy and to prosper,

then I have only to rely upon God to lead me and guide me. I have only to believe that the kingdom is the Lord's.

Why would I doubt? We do because we do not see it. We see only the manifestation of the spirit.

My existence is because of God. Why would He not take care of me? I see Him as He is: a rewarder of those who diligently seek Him.

All that I have needed, His hands have provided. Charity never fails. He loves this body too.

The battle is the Lord's. It is His kingdom.

He has control of His kingdom; it is His glory and power. Start in the Spirit and end in the Spirit. Then and only then will we be happy. God, when we are weak You are strong.

When fear enters our mind, we cast out fear because Jesus overcame that fear. God's words will put aside those thoughts. They will dissolve, they will vanish, and they will disappear.

We hate to do things, but we do them out of greed.

I hate to go to work, but I need the money.

Teach me to love and to do what I love.

Show me the way, Lord.

God is in each one of us, He does not want us to be bogged down with religion. Salvation and religion are two different things.

He wants us to be free.

To live and to love and to do good to others.

My heart cries out:

What would You have me to do with what You have given me?

How do I portray You in this life? What do I do? No! What can You do through me to magnify your grace and truth?

Lucifer, you have taken a back seat, so I know you are not sitting in the temple of God ever again. God is love; God is truth.

"And we know that all things work together for good to them that love God, to them who are called according to His purpose" (Romans 8:28).

How do I bless Your people? We do not worry about whether we can do the job.

It is not us doing it; it is God, and God is able to accomplish that which He has started. Is not that wonderful that brings peace and joy. You know the way for Your people. Go high and be lifted with Him.

It is God who works through us to will and to do of His good pleasure. Be holy in the mind and be lifted today. Sin shall no more have dominion over us. God will see that it accomplishes what it was sent to do.

We can have peace in knowing God is at the helm. We are servants of God. We do whatsoever our Father says, knowing all things work together for good. God knows all things.

"Finally, brethren, whatsoever things are true, whatsoever things are honest, whatsoever things are just, whatsoever things are pure, whatsoever things are lovely, whatsoever things are of good report; if there be any virtue, and if there be any praise, think on these things" (Philippians 4:8).

God knows the route I should go. I do not know the route. Think peace and be lifted with God this day. Have faith and be lifted with Him. Mountains shall move. I say mountains shall move.

God is omnipotent and knows all things. He is all things to all people.

How do I help Your people, a needy people, a merciful people? How do I set Your people free, wholly free for all to see?

27

My Prayer #2

Do You want me to serve you spontaneously, to give as You have given to me? May Your blessings be heaped up and running over as we give to Your people.

I know You are making a way for Your children.

I am free to write because I want to help Your people.

Not because of the money, not because of the fame, not because of the power.

But because I know there is help in life-giving words.

By every word that proceeded forth from Your mouth, God, I am sure there is a way each one can help Your people.

As You are high and lifted Your mercy will flow.

God, I believe You shall move mountains each day for us. Your spirit said it, and I believe it.

We are the temple of God. The King has a kingdom. The King has servants dedicated to the King in His kingdom. The King is the ruler.

No one else.

The King's words rule, no questions asked. To seek the kingdom of God and His righteousness is complete trust in His Word, which is final.

We are the temple, and God's spirit dwells in His temple. God is love, and love dwells in the temple. Peace and joy are in the Holy Spirit. Seek peace, joy, and comfort. Be free to have peace, joy, and comfort. No sorrow added. No condemnation, no doubts, no unbelief, and no torment.

28

My Prayer #3

God, I sure do thank You for opening my eyes to the truth. We are Your children, and we need not be afraid. We can take dominion over the darkness and principalities. We know and believe and are persuaded that nothing shall separate us from You. We can take dominion over the powers that would cause harm to us, our family, and our friends. In Your name.

29

Love Is Freedom

Many may not like the way God delivers His people. For it will be by His spirit, as we bind the enemy of our souls.

Be strong in the Lord and in the power of His might. We shall have satisfying minds. All things are possible to those who believe.

The best part of it all is that we realize we have the power to say, "I will make the right choice, and the right choice will be made."

We are not helpless creatures. We are strong and mighty, knowing that we have power that was given to us from the foundation of the Earth.

God made us in His image. Until we exercise that truth, we are most miserable.

Being raised with so much fear has left scars on my life that have finally been erased. I have come above them. I know that God dwells within me and that I have nothing to fear. Just like the Word reads: fear not!

I want you to know today that there is a way that seems right, and there is a way that is right. I have come to show you the way that is right, and that way is the way of truth and the life. He dwells within us to rule and reign within our lives.

I cannot believe how good I am feeling this day. I know I have nothing to fear.

"For I know in whom I have believed; and am persuaded that He is able to keep that which I have committed unto Him against that day" (2 Timothy 1:12).

We know that nothing shall separate us from our God, who dwells within. We are creatures of circumstance. We believe whatever is told to us by somebody who says he knows.

We do not bother to consider the situation for ourselves; we would rather be lazy and not search. Or we do not know to search for ourselves. I have found that there is a way that is right, and that way is the right way to go. There is a God, and we all have God within us in some form.

Either we have Him still as a child, or in bondage down in Egypt, or hanging on the cross, or in the grave, or resurrected, or sitting on the throne.

We need to search Him for ourselves and not be satisfied with second had knowledge.

We have Him within us in some shape or form. How comforting to know that there is freedom in having a living God dwell within. He does not expect more than what we can believe. We all have love within us so that love is that measure of faith that is born in each of us. That love will lead us and guide us in the right direction.

30

Mercy: A Sign of Weakness or Strength

One of the best ways to consider the future is to reevaluate the past.

Where there is fear, you will find hate and rebellion.

Children rebel a lot of the time because they are not shown consideration and fairness by their parents. They are not an appliance that you can switch on and off. The first time your children get into trouble, are they given a chance to explain. It really hurts when we are accused wrongfully by those who are closest to us. Was he disowned by family and friends, or was there someone he could turn to for advice and comfort?

We are indebted to one another and should love each other. When that love is not shown, then there is rebellion. We strike back one way or another. Love will cover the bad in those we meet and bring forth the good. There is a little light of love in each one of us. It can be made to burn brighter, or it can be smothered out until it no longer shines.

We put people in prisons without walls. We put barriers between us that guns and ammunition cannot break down. It could be that not being able to forgive has separated more loved ones than anything else known.

Fear? Afraid of what? Many are bound by fear. They are caught in its clutches. People who are afraid cannot help themselves. They try not to be afraid, the same as an addict tries to refrain, but they are held under that spell. Can we not find mercy in our hearts for those who are afraid? Showing mercy to the weak makes us to be stronger individuals. Showing mercy is a sign of strength, not weakness.

31

A Love Not Known Before

I have never known such love as this, that He lays down His life for His friends.

Jesus found me when I was just a little girl, afraid and feeling all alone.

Jesus began to woo me, and tell me of His great love, and show me there has never been a love such as His love.

It is a love that sees no evil in us. He conquered evil for us. He looks at our hearts. He conquered all we will ever face. Although our minds will be the last thing to embrace that truth, it is truth, and it will stand.

Down through the years, with all the aches and pains and conflicts and heartaches, never once did He leave me or forsake me or make me feel bad. He was always there to lift my load and whisper sweet music to my ears.

Sometimes He has had to repeat His goodness to me. Year after year, He has had to repeat the same thing to me. Most people do not want to repeat the same thing twice. Never once did He not want to help me. That is all He knows: to help and heal.

I have never known a love such as this. God loves us with a love I cannot even comprehend, a love that has never failed.

When I am not good to myself, He is there to show me the way. When I mistreat someone, He gently shows me how to do better.

He has walked every step that I will ever take.

He overcame everything that comes against me.

He was victorious and knows what it takes to endure.

While growing up as a carpenter; He studied the Bible and wrote it all on His heart. When in the synagogue, He quoted the Word. He was only twelve, but He was rooted and grounded in the Word. He lived the Word while here on Earth. He used the Word to overcome His enemies. The Word did not fail Him. He did not try the Word to see whether it would work. He knew that the Word would work. He staked His life on the Word. He gave His life for the Word. We are afraid to rely on the Word. "Speak the Word only and my servant shall be healed" (Matthew 8:8). We are afraid to speak the Word, afraid we do not believe it enough. The power is in the Word. He was sure it would not fail.

Sometimes we must get out in deep waters to swim, or to find out we can swim.

There was not a doubt in Jesus mind. He knew the Word would work. He believed His Father.

When He needed reinforcement, He got away from the crowd and prayed to His Father. He said He did not do anything except what His Father told Him to do.

He fought His earthly mind as we fight our earthly minds. That is our cross. We have an elder brother who overcame the cross. Therefore, we know of a surety we will too.

Lead us not into temptation but deliver us from evil—the evil of not believing His Word.

Fear, doubt, and unbelief cause condemnation, which is our enemy. It was Adam and Eve's enemy too. These are the sins against our spirits. They come from our minds, and that is what we struggle with.

Rest assured that God's words will put them to flight. His words are spirit, and they do not return void. They accomplish what they are sent to do.

I have struggled with my weight for at least fifty years. I sought God about it all the time, and He would show me the answer, but it was too simple. I did not believe it. I kept seeking day in and day out. Sometimes I thought I had found the answer, and then it would fail. Many, many times I did that down through the years. I wrote many pages, seeking God for the answer. The answer He showed me did not match what my mind was telling me, so I did not believe it. I simply could not grasp it.

He would show me how to take responsibility for my actions and love myself enough to only do good to myself. That is the way God loves me: with an everlasting love, a love that would not fail me. Never once did He condemn me for not grasping what He was telling me.

My mind was telling me if I took responsibility for my actions, then I was doing it by "might and power" and not by the spirit, as the Word reads. The enemy knows the Word too.

Then one day, His Word finally got through to me. "I can do all things through Christ which strengthens me" (Philippians 4:13). I can do all things. Me! With God's strength, by His Word.

I can care enough for myself to do what is the best thing for me, to love myself like God loves me. That is a love that does not fail me, an everlasting love. You look out for those you love. You cherish them, care for them, and answer their needs—just like God does! It is not easy to change, but when it is for our good, we can do it. Sometimes we take care of everyone else besides ourselves. Who is going to take care of us? We are.

I have learned many, many wonderful words of wisdom by my searching for the truth. I would start out seeking how to lose weight and end up finding wonderful truths in His Word.

My seeking to lose weight was like a "thorn in the flesh," like the apostle Paul spoke. It kept me on my knees. God knew there were more important truths I needed to learn. By seeking God, I was more than rewarded.

I have never known such love. I find no fault in Him. Even though I could not grasp what He was showing me about responsibility, He never quit leading and guiding me into His truths.

He knew His love would not fail me.

Someday when this life is over, I can truthfully say, "Jesus led me all the way."

He never got tired of me crying and begging for the truth. Not once did He rebuke me. His arms were always open. He did not seem to ever see me as being weak and full of unbelief. He knew His love would cover all.

I am so thankful for the experience I have had seeking God.

Through many heartaches, failures, conflicts, and tears, it has been worth it all to find out how great His love is toward His children.

Taking time to be thankful makes the bumps seem a little smaller.

Being thankful keeps faith alive. It is a time to be thankful. A time to remember the days gone by. A time to reflect and breathe a sigh. A time to blot out the troubles that surround us. A time to renew our faith in others. A time to say thanks and give a helping hand. A time to realize the real values in life have not changed.

A time to give hope and trust again. A time to search what makes for happiness. A time to look within oneself, being thankful. This is what brings great wealth.

How important is the breath of life? With the breath of life, we are engulfed by the spirit of God. We became living souls. We became children of God. That measure of faith was implanted within us. That seed is to be nourished and guarded with our lives. For that is our lives—it is the breath of life.

When Mary conceived with Jesus, it was by the spirit.

When we receive the breath of life, it is totally by the spirit. With that breath of life, we are given eternal life.

When our bodies are gone, our spirits live on. Our spirits are the pearl of great price.

If we do not allow the thought, then actions will not follow. These are life-giving words to learn and speak. Our spirits are greater than our flesh.

His Word has dominion over everything that comes against us. Jesus used the Word. When our minds and spirits are in harmony, then we are free from stress. Feelings that are against love are powers and principalities that need to be conquered.

Our thinking puts to death God's thinking, and then we are left destroyed. God has showed us love; we know what it feels like.

It is food for life, natural and spiritual.

We are the temple of His spirit. Speak the Word and see it come to pass, loving ourselves to do what is right. Love does not pressure. We choose love. A love that never wavers, never turns. An unconditional love.

We need to return to our first love, to become as little children with complete trust. Completely trust yourself to do what is best for you. We can learn to love ourselves with love that will never let us down.

No matter how badly we want to do something, we will not allow ourselves to do that thing if it is not good for us. If it will make our spirit sad, if it will make us feel like we have failed, if it makes us wish we could have done differently, then even though in the past we have given into this temptation, this time we will not do that. We will love ourselves too much to allow that to make us unhappy. We can declare our freedom. We cannot do it on our own. We need His Word.

"Present your bodies a living sacrifice; Holy and acceptable unto God, which is your reasonable service" (Romans 12:1).

We have not given of ourselves: our minds, thoughts, hearts, our souls, and our bodies.

Love has not been our motivator. Fear has been our conqueror. We have let fear, in whatever shape we used, to rob us of love.

That shape could be by drawing away, hiding, feeling unworthy. There is fear of failure, doubting yourself, fear of giving of yourself, being frozen by fear, being disillusioned by doubt, being sure of failure.

Work, that you may have to give. It is better to give than to receive. You cannot give if you do not have it to give. Therefore, if you have it to give, then you are blessed. Before you give and after you give, you are blessed.

Love day and night. Fill your life with love. Eat it, sleep it, live it. For when we love ourselves like God loves us, we will do only what is good for us.

32

God Speaks, but Who Is Listening?

I am in you, and you in Me.
I am you; you are Me.
Where am I? But in you.
I made you in My image.
If you are the image of Me,
Then I am the same as you.
I and you, and you and Me.
You are Me, and I am you.
Can you honestly believe that?
Can you think it not robbery to be equal with Me?
Can you believe that?
Can you say I and the Father are one?
My flesh was crucified,
I laid down My body and came to dwell within you.
Heaven and earth shall pass-away,
But my words shall not pass-away.
I am drawing you unto Myself.
Where I am, there you shall be also.
Whatever you do, I do.
Whatever you think, I think.
Whatever you believe to be true shall come to pass.
Because I dwell within you, and you in Me we two are one.
I say My love shall cleanse sickness all out of your body.
You shall know no pain or the pains of death.
You shall be cleansed and made ever whole.

33

What Did Jesus Do?

What did Jesus do while here on Earth? His meat was to do the Father's will. He ministered unto the sick and oppressed. He declared the Word. He knew to do good, and He did it.

He had a mission to accomplish. What was the mission? Save the world from their sins of unbelief. We are spirit, we are flesh.

"How is it that ye sought me? Wist thee not that I must needs be about my Father's business" (Luke 2:49).

What was His Father's business? Loving and caring. Speaking the truth. Redeeming us back to love.

34

Build upon Your Own Foundation

Do not build on someone else's foundation. If you are a builder, you will be the one to dig the foundation. Then you will be the one to build upon that foundation, not someone's ideas or dreams. You will build on the foundation that is clear to you as you read His Word.

Jesus is the chief cornerstone. If He is not the cornerstone, then your foundation will be weak. It will then have joints in the mortar that are weak and will not be able to stand the fire.

Know for sure you will be tested and tried. If you are in it for a big name, money, prestige, or fame, then do not be surprised when the foundation crumbles.

Jesus's will shall be our constant aim. He does not share His glory.

35

Our Talents

Each of our talents is unique indeed. Lifting
the fallen, strengthening the weak.
Preparing the way of true worship at His feet.
Nudging and guiding, willing to lead His
people out of bondage of fear and deceit.
Ever waiting and watching prepared to relieve
the aches and the pains of hate and greed.
God is in each one of our lives, showing
us the way to be loving and wise.
Gentleness and long-suffering, is the name of the game,
not pushing or shoving to make for us a name.
Waiting and watching, ever wanting to please, the
creator of the universe who takes away our dis-ease.
Struggling and striving, never satisfied it seems.
Always wanting something more,
continually seeking an open door.
Being content with what we possess
Will rid our lives of envy, bitterness, and stress.
Each one of us is unique, if our talents
we use. Lifting the fallen
And not drawing back, to refuse.

36

Your Mind

Our minds need to be strengthened until they believe all things are possible.

Think with the spiritual mind. What is your mind? It is spirit, and it is truth. With my mind, all things are possible. Conflict is in my mind.

I see what is in my mind. It is conflict. Conflicting thoughts about what I should do.

God wants us to believe that all things are possible. We strengthen our minds by listening to His words, which are spirit and life.

We are in bondage regarding what we believe, what we have been taught.

How do I go out of my fleshly mind? Out of my way of thinking? How do I move out of my way of thinking? My mind is fearful. My mind is doubtful. My mind is full of unbelief. What is truth? My mind is not against flesh and blood. It is against the spirit. My mind is against spiritual things.

37

Our Spirit Speaks to Us: Make a Way

I come to make a way where there is no way.
Hear you Me.
I am the way maker.
Lift your eyes unto the hills.
It is where your help comes from.
Your help is in the hills.
The hills of great glory.
You are troubled.
Your thinking is troubling; it is not Godly.
Complete trust is Godly.
Therefore, you do not trust Me fully.
Your mind will not let you.
You do not think you are worthy.
Your thinking blocks out all worthiness.
Your thinking will not let you partake of the tree of life.
My words are spirit, and they are life.
Humans cannot live by bread alone,
But by every word that proceeds out of My mouth.
My people shall not perish,
For My words are spirit, and they are life.
Peace I give unto you, not as the world gives unto you.
Then there is a way that is right.
Come, and I will make a way where there is no way.
Come, and I will make a way for you.
My mercy holds.

"Take my yoke upon you and learn of me. For
I am meek and lowly at heart you shall find
rest unto your soul" (Matthew 11:29).
It is mercy that holds My people.
Let not your heart be troubled and let not it be afraid.
Mercy in the mind, coming out of darkness
into My marvelous light of day.
Let My people go.
My people are in bondage to their way of thinking.
My people are afraid of living.
They are afraid of what they have been told.
My people are a free people though they do not know it.
Let My people go.
Set My people free,
Free for people to see.
My people need to be set free, to be holy and be
lifted with Me, for I am meek and lowly in heart,
and you shall find rest unto your soul.
Let My people go.
Go, I say go.
Set My people free, Free for people to see.
My people are a free people, but they do not know it.
My mercy holds My people.
Love lifts My people; let My people go.
Love lifts, there is a way that seems right,
And then there is a way that is right.
Come unto Me.

38

Quotes to Remember

Proceed and do what you know to do. You can be successful in all things.

Boredom results from not doing the duty at hand.

Wisdom comes by seeking truth.

Procrastination creates many dis-eases:
Boredom, overeating, frustration, anxiety, depression, and oppression.
We eat trying to take away that gnawing inside of us
That comes from not doing what we know to do.
Negative thoughts are against our health.
A healthy mind needs to be kept in action.
Why can't we just be ourselves?
Why can't we yawn, stretch, and laugh?
Why do we always rush?
Always thinking we must do this and that?

Satisfaction in your work is worth striving to attain.
Only then can you be truly contented.

Dissatisfaction is discouraged, but it should never be discouraged.
When dissatisfaction is used as a stepping-stone,
Great avenues can emerge.

Writing is a creative form of life.

Take time to listen to the voice crying in the wilderness within.
Keep your head.
Do not be disillusioned by vain thoughts
Puffing you up, only to let you down.
Truth will hold you steady and will never let you down.

Do not fear to live,
For only by living will you find life.

Do not fear to be yourself; there is only one you.
Seeing our own faults will help us stop seeing the faults of others.

If is a stumbling block that only you can remove.

Peace stills the storm.

Love is as precious as good health, something you cannot neglect.

Stand up and be counted; it is the only way to free your soul.
Strengthen whatever potentials you may possess.
Whatever is worth having is still worth working for.

Nothing can stop us if we are determined.

Truth leads upward and forward at the same time.

There is a way that seems right.

There is a way that is right.

If we would be happy and successful,
Search out every opportunity that comes our way.

A way can be made.
It only takes determination.
When the idea comes, plant it in rich soil; do not push it aside.
Water it well, give it thought.
Make plans, watch it spring forth.
Anything worth having is worth waiting for.

Perseverance seems to be the key to finding oneself.

We have tried to change circumstance by thinking there is a way,
Only to find out there is no satisfactory way.
May we be able to accept that fact and not let it pull us down.
Learn to pursue another course.
Learning by our past experiences, even though failure comes;
we are the better for trying.
We have gained knowledge that we could have never learned
any other way.

Detours can be used to better chart our course.

Stopping for a season can be a blessing in disguise.

Success stems from real concern.

What we make of our lives
Depends upon how much we have invested.

An abused friendship soon dwindles.

We are responsible for our feelings.

Our minds are as a computer, playing back what was
programmed.

Life is short; spend it well.

Look for the good in others, and it will make you a more considerate person.

Facing up to the truth is a sure way of improvement.

Be frank and sincere when offering suggestions.

Life is for real, so watch the games.

Criticism is the forerunner of condemnation.

Hard work makes dreams come true.

Fear conquers; love motivates.

Truth dispels fear.

Hope brings results.

Failures can be turned into stepping-stones.

Fear binds, truth sets free.

Time has a way of healing.

Patience will win out.

Love is a workable force.

Be a good listener, for you can move many mountains for someone else.

Giving of oneself is true love.

Sharing is a two-way blessing.

Fear of failure can cause hate.

Caring is loving.

Judgment should only be practiced on oneself.
Unspoken love is waste.

Clubs can become rackets.

Faith in humankind is contagious.

Love may not seem to be the formula, but it is always the right
solution.

Joy comes only through victory.

Hate destroys; love heals.

An open mind to the ideas of others will help free your mind
to think more clearly.

Some have a need to believe certain fantasies because they do
not have the strength to face the truth.
Concentration can only reap great rewards.

Looking behind the face we present can be very eye-opening.

I have but one life to give; may I not let fear hamper my giving.

You freely give when you forgive. You are understanding your neighbor as yourself.

Finding oneself is sometimes a struggle for a lifetime, not taking time to listen to the voice within.
We have only to seek peace, to find it.
We have only to knock on the door of peace, to have it open unto us.

We have only to lay aside our fears, to listen to the still, small voice that has been here from the beginning, waiting to be heard.
When all else has failed us, we are complete in ourselves.

We need the Holy spirit to teach us. We have the necessary tools to find peace.

When we have found peace, we then can lend a helping hand to those who are steeped in bondage, to help hasten their escape from their own minds.
From their own thinking,
From their traditions,
From their fears,
From their doubts,
From their rites and rituals.
The warfare is in our minds.
Our minds are the firing line, the front line of battle.
We need to choose a few stones to slay the giant and make sure they hit the mark.
Only then can we be truly contented.
We can be brainwashed by the crowd. We should look at the crowd before conforming. Their hang-ups may be even greater than our own.

We do not listen, and therefore we do not learn.

Perfect peace comes from within.

Pressures can be great when we are not certain of the outcome.

We all share one thing in common, life.
There is much fear in ignorance.

An educated fool is one that has ruled out common sense.

If you do not roll with the punches, you may get badly bruised.
We all fight the same battles.

Violence is learned.

There is no way you can help a person if you do not care.

Rebellion can lead to disaster.

If you do not bend, you may break.

Do not let fears and doubts hold you back.
Press on through,
They are usually imaginary.
Be prepared for the best in life.
Then the rough spots will not seem so bad.

Time and patience are all it takes to tackle a problem.
Fear is blind; faith brings sight.

39

Love and Hate

Love takes time.
Hate rushes on.
Love looks down and lends the helping hand.
Hate overlooks and tightens the band.
Love and hate: both are very real and strong.
One is right, the other wrong.
One is kind, the other distraught.
One is contaminated, the other is pure.
One fails, the other secures.
Love and hate remember they are real.
One can cause sickness, the other can heal.
Love will lift, while hate puts down.
One will swim, while the other drowns.
Love and hate at the tug-of-war.
Love will win out, while hate roars.
Love is not narrow-minded.
Love is open, love is pure.
Love reaches out, it does not hold back.
Love sees beyond the face of doubt.
Loves fragrance is sweet and warming and kind.
Melts even the coldest heart when fear would bind.
Love says there is a way,
Even in the darkest hour, love is truly a stay.
Where is God? He seems so far out.
Where is love? Then take that route.
When you find love, there God will be.

For God is love and shall be through eternity.
"You mean I just must love, and do away with hate
To know the God that is so great?"
That is what He says, for love is strong.
It overcomes evil and downs wrong.
That is what God is all about: to love thy neighbor as thyself.
If I can help my neighbor, then I am working within God's plan.
Love tugs at our hearts each day.
By a little child, with the broken toy at play.
Maybe just a kind word would turn away that wrath
From the tormented one, fallen along the path.
Love does not fail, but there is a price to pay.
The price is giving of ourselves each day.
As you give out, you somehow get more.
For His love is waiting at an open door.

40

A Slave to Love

A slave to love—
What better master to have?
To lead and guide in work or play.
A slave to love.
The bonds are great.
With love and mercy bound around our neck,
A slave to love.
An opportunity never known,
For kindness is reaped when love is sown.
Love is not one-sided, it is not narrow-minded, nor rude.
Love is blind to the faults of others,
Sees only the hungry soul of his brother.
Love does not condemn the symptoms
It goes straight to the wound.
Love overlooks the ugly stains
And protects the bud until it blooms.
Let love and mercy be your weapons of war
When contention and strife stand at your door.
I love my people.
I would not that you be hungry and not fed.
I would not that the enemy comes in like a flood to overthrow you.
I would not that you be tormented day and night.
I would not that you be the children of the devil.
I would not that you be sick and poor.
I come that you might have life and have it more abundantly.

And I would that you be in health and prosper,
Even as your soul prospers.
For love is the key that opens the door,
For a greater life than you have known before.

41

God Is by My Side

I feel
What you feel.
How do I feel what you feel?
I dwell within.
When you hurt,
I hurt.
When you bleed,
I bleed.
When your heart aches,
Mine aches
When you rejoice,
I rejoice.
When you have faith
We join forces.
How can you fail?
With Me on your side.
I am your friend.
I fail not.
What looks like failures
Are only stepping-stones
To something better.
Pick up the pieces,
Put them back together.
Look for life, and ye shall find it.
You were born
With a measure of faith.

Let that seed be born in you.
Nourish that seed.
Let it blossom and come forth
To full stature,
Until I am Lord of your life.
I am life,
I am peace,
I am understanding.
I am whatever you have need of.

42

God's Love Is Contagious

My joy is contagious.
My victory is won.
I search only what is good.
I care.
I am mercy.
I am strong.
I bring peace.
I know the way, and I know the right way.
I make you to shine.
I have no boundaries.
I free the mind.
I give wings to the soul.
I lift the spirit.
I bring you good tidings of great joy to all people.
I dedicate, I concentrate, I perform.
I bear witness of the truth.
I am workable.
I am pliable.
I have feelings.
I have real emotions.
I dwell in every human being.
I know who will finish the race.
I am always uplifting; I never condemn.
I magnified the good in whatever I do.
I wait.
I give a good feeling.

I can swim.
I can bend and not break.
I come in all shapes and sizes.
I can be felt.
I can be seen.
I take a chance.
I do not draw back.
I give the benefit of the doubt.
I go the second mile.
I lend a helping hand.
I feed the hungry.
I give to the poor.
I have what you are searching for.
I see the storm brewing.
I mend the brokenhearted.
I put the pieces together.
I am the missing link in the chain.
I break down the hedges,
Tear down the fences.
I free the mind.
I give wings to the soul.
My laughter is rich and mellow.
I ring out good tidings of great joy to all people.
I bear witness of the truth.
I have emotions.
I win all.
I am the victor from the start.
I never condemn.
I always understand.
I see only the good in others.
I have a listening ear.
I deliver you from your enemies.

I make a way for your escape.
I will hold you when all else fails.
I take away your suffering.
I cast out evil imaginations.
I rid you of spite and from degradation,
Take away your pride.
I set your face toward the goal.
I never look back.
I see the needy.
I helped the forlorn.
I am strength.
I fail not.
I am the messenger of peace.
I know the right way.
I do not stumble.
I make you beautiful.
I make you shine as the stars.
I see no walls.

43

Be Proud, America! March On!

America! America!
The land of the free!
Freedom from slavery and
Freedom to vote!
Freedom to think and speak as we belong.
It is a blessing to lie down at night and not hear
Bombs blasting and sirens screaming.
We can move about freely, doing what we desire to do.
We can fulfill our dreams, accomplish our hopes and desires.
And reach out to help and be willing to be helped.
America! America! The home of the brave.
Develop courage to attain the goals we have set
So, we can leave a heritage of love.
Develop courage to be what our conscious bids us to be.
We know that brotherhood stems from our own self-respect.
We are a nation of freedom-loving leaders and troops.
May our hearts, prayers, and actions reflect
Gratitude to all who dedicated their lives
toward protecting our liberties.
Courage is simple faith that is coupled
with works to sustain us.
"Oh! say can you see by the dawn's early light?"
What do we see for America?
Freedom is meant for one and all.
Freedom was not meant to harm our neighbors.
With liberty comes responsibility.

Look within to the courage to be free.
When discrimination is present, we belittle the cause.
Commitment will give us many happy returns America.
Stand tall, America! March on!
Many have left their footprints on the sands of time.
Their courage and faith make way for our tomorrows.
The horizon is even more challenging as it lights our path.
Be proud, America! March on!

44

Help Keep America Free

If you were informed that the survival of this nation
depended upon you, and you had only
twenty-four hours to give advice,
what would you tell this generation?
What message would you want them to remember?
What survival tools would you give them?
What would be your guidelines? What would be utmost?
Would you teach them to be greedy?
Would they get the impression to take, take, take?

Feel what your child feels.
Take time to suffer with him, developing his worth.
Searching until you get answers.
Then our children will know that solutions can be found
and will not give up in despair. Each of us can
fill a void until eventually it will take form.

How did we arrive at where we are today?
Pioneers developed new land, discovered new
territories, ventured by faith and courage.
Took no thought for their lives, knowing they
had a job to do, and went about doing it.
Willing to give, give, and give. We need to
replenish the Earth. We need pioneers, people
who will dare venture beyond the ordinary.
Our subscription to live runs out if it is not renewed.
Each life is important.

Each has been endued with a special mission.
No one else can fulfill that mission.
Each is given a space of time to fulfill that duty.
Some take their talents and multiply, while
others hide the talent, and it is wasted.
We will never know what may have been accomplished.
What, impact that life could have had upon all generations.
We can stop this degeneration.

We may have to sweat, get our hands
dirty, and maybe take a backseat.
We can still carve out a good way of life.
We do not have to be self-destructive;
we can get off that course.
We can fight for what we believe.
We can put the Word work back into our vocabulary.
We can know the satisfaction in accomplishments.
We can give instead of take.
We can leave a heritage that we can be proud of
as we enrich the lives of our children and their children.
A life that will not fail them.

We tend to emphasize the evil instead of
exhausting our efforts on all the good.
Good can overcome evil.
God dwelling within, being the greater force.
Before we will see the results,
we must act!
We can be part of the solution,
not part of the problem.
Stand up! Be counted! Bring back harmony in the family!
Just as in our government! Freedom in our land!

A link in the chain is weakened when we say we do not care.
There is something each one of us can do.
We may never make headlines! We can
do what is in our power to do.

We all have a part in electing competent leaders,
honest men and women who really care
about the future of this nation.
Who will work until the wee hours of
the night, to sustain justice?
At a time when it seems few cares.
Let us find those few and lend a supportive hand.
We can all know a nation of liberty and justice for all.
We must elaborate on justice and not give air to crime,
finding ways to prevent crime. This is a
local issue, a nationwide call,
beginning within us.

We may have taken the path of least resistance; if so, in the
end we have only ourselves to blame. One vote does make
a difference. One cloud can keep the sun from shining.
Also, an outstretched hand can keep a soul from drowning.
What happened to the people who lived and died for a
cause? Showing forth integrity that sits men's souls aflame.
May we hear the beat of their drums.
Our nation's heritage.

One nation undivided. We are part of this nation.
We are its arms, its legs, its hands, its
brain, and the life that flows.
Not forgetting the backbone: the strength to stand or fall.
We are our brothers' keeper,

when it is in our power to do so. We can introduce
the word *caring* into our vocabulary again.

We can pray, keeping faith, working to fulfill our
hopes, and expending our energy into action. While
we make the heritage, let us leave a workable force.

45

Anxiety

Our Unseen Enemy. God communicates with His children through His spirit that dwells within their hearts and minds.

I worked in a clinic for several years. At noontime, I would answer the phone and make appointments for the counselors while they ate lunch.

One noon the phone rang, and it was a gentleman who wanted to talk immediately with someone. I ask if there was anything I could do because all the counselors were at lunch. He began to tell about the nightmares and dreams that were causing anxiety, that were taking over his life, since he got home from the war. He had lost his wife, his children, and everything that meant anything to him. He had made a mess of his life. He felt like he had no place to turn to for help. As a soldier, he was haunted by the horrible killings he had been involved in. Day and night, he was tormented. He could not find peace. He could not find forgiveness because he did not believe he deserved to be forgiven.

I reminded him that God forgives all. All he had to do is ask for forgiveness and God is there to completely forgive. He only had to believe that and forgive himself. He needed to be reminded he was doing what he was sent to do in the war. He did not have a choice when he was there. He was carrying all the blame of what had happened in battle with him. His burden was too heavy to carry. He felt he had lost all. He thanked me for listening to him and hung up the phone.

Later that afternoon, one of the counselors told me they got a call from a gentleman wanting them to thank that lady who had talked to him at noon. He was going to talk to his wife, and he felt his life was going to be turned around. He now had hope, because a heavy load had been lifted, and he now felt he may have a second chance in life. It is amazing what happens when we ask for forgiveness and believe that we have been forgiven.

God's Word states that His words will not return to void. His Word will accomplish what it is sent to do.

Fear. I would like to share what I felt when I had anxiety attacks this spring. Only God's word helped me make it through the day, and through the night. This was so frightening I wondered if I would ever be myself again. To anyone who has ever had an anxiety attack I can say I understand the feeling. The enormous feeling of not being able to breathe. It was as if something had taken control of my life. I did not have control of my thinking! I was afraid I might die. There were times that the tightness in my chest was so bad that I felt bruised. This went on for days. One morning I got out of bed with anxiety, tightness in my chest, and shortness of breath.

Anxiety was something entirely foreign to me. After a couple hours with no relief I called my daughter at work and she came home. I had the signs of a heart attack, so we called 911 and I was taken to the hospital. I was given the entire rounds of test and kept overnight to take a stress test the next morning. The test was fine, so I was sent home. I did not know what a big battle it was going to be to undo the fear in my mind. This was a real feeling. It was so strong I could not battle it. I needed reinforcement from my spirit to fight the natural mind, which was coming against me.

His Word. I began to rely on God's Word. His Word helped me every time—sometimes not as quickly as I would like, but He always came on time. I had lots to learn about trusting His Word. I learned more about feeding my spirit. The Bible reads, "Man can't live by bread alone; but by every word that proceeds out of the mouth of God" (Matthew 4:4). I learned to draw upon His Word. His Word brought life to me. My fears and anxieties became less. His words were a treasure of hidden love.

His Word will never leave me and will never forsake me. He comes to make a way where there is no way. He always makes a way. He never turns away from me. If I feel like I am away from God, it is my mind that causes me to feel that way. He will never leave me. For God is peace, rest, and goodness. He also says His words will not return to void. They will do what they are sent to do. It took several weeks before I was completely free from those thoughts. When I called on God to help me, He gave me His words to sustain me.

These fearful thoughts may seem like they came overnight, but there is a way out. Rest assured they will leave as you quote God's words of comfort. Sometimes we may need to say them out loud, to cry out for help, because the fears seem so strong. They are holding on with a tight grip. As we cry out, they will loosen their hold. God will give you strength to stand against your enemy. The enemy comes to steal, to kill, and to destroy. God's words give only life, love, mercy, and comfort.

Making a Way. He gives life more abundantly. There is a way that seems right, and then there is a way that is right. I had to keep searching until I found the way that is right. God can teach me His way. God knows what I need and what I need to believe.

I am not happy unless I am doing what You would have me do. I praise You for that Lord, for Your mercy, for Your goodness, for Your kindness, and for Your generosity.

If God can take care of the birds, He can keep me in peace. I have only to keep my mind and spirit turned to Him. God comes that I might have life and life more abundantly. God's words are life, peace, rest, and comfort.

You know everything. You are willing to give Your words of peace to take away the fears that dwell within my thoughts and feelings.

He took away my fears. Every time, He simply does not fail. Sometimes I cried out several times before I was able to calm myself to listen to what God had to say. His words did not fail me. He came and made a way where seemingly, seemingly there was no way. God came and made a way in the darkest night, when things were crashing in on me, when there was no light to shine upon my pathway. He came and made a way. Every time, every time, He came and made a way. He comforted me with His Word.

Does God Really Care? Does He really care for me? Yes, He does. His temple is within us. He lives within us. His spirit is life, peace, and comfort. He does not come to discourage us. He does not come to find fault with us. He does not cause us to feel inferior or to think that we have failed. His words are speaking to us. We are not being quiet enough to hear his voice. He always comes to make a way where there is no way. It may seem like there is no way. He says His words will come to our remembrance when we need the word. As we read His Word, it brings deliverance.

Nobody cares, nobody will help me, no one will put their arms around me! God cares. He is making a way for His people this day. He is making a way. You are His life, love, mercy, strength, goodness, long-suffering, gentleness, kindness, and glory. We need to learn to listen because He is there. When we read the Word and put His words in our heart, we can use those words of life.

If we are having trouble believing, we should ask God to help our unbelief. He gives strength to the weak. He bears us up on wings of eagles. We can run and not be weary, we can walk and not faint. Teach me, Lord to wait. We must wait and believe and quote His words of life until they are real to us, for His words are our lifeline. Peace can sweep over us when we least expect it, and we can breathe again.

King David could have called on many counselors when he was in trouble. He hid God's Word in his heart because he knew where his help came from. He found peace, rest, and comfort. Then he knew he could rely on God's words.

Sometimes the fears seem so strong that they are holding in a tight grip, like claws. Cry out for reinforcement. You mean business and are trusting God to give you grace to stand against your enemy. God's words give only life, love, mercy, and comfort. Fight for this and do not give up. The enemy has tried to destroy you, but you know that now, so you know where the enemy is. It is your thinking keeping you bound. Little by little, you are changing your thinking to believe God is life. It is our thinking that needs to be renewed to think life for us. We learn to think on things that are peaceful, gentle, and kind, with long-suffering and patience. Just remember His words put the enemy to flight. He told His enemy to get behind Him. You have the greater power because God lives within you.

Being Thankful. Thank God, for we now know our enemy and can truthfully come against the enemy. His Word states, "Let us come before His presence with thanksgiving, and make a joyful noise unto him with Psalms. For the lord is a great God, and a great King above all Gods" (Psalm. 95:2–4). Whatever we have been reaching for to try to calm our fears, it may seem to have worked for a season. We had nothing else to lean on. We were grappling and were doing all we knew to do. Then we were left helpless again and again. We get into God's Word, learn of His love, learn of His goodness, and learn that He really does care for us. He is with us continually. He knows our sorrows. He knows our anxieties. Then we are so thankful. We may torture ourselves from things that have happened in the past. We need to forgive ourselves, because if we could have done differently, we would have. God forgives everything we confess with faith, believing.

When we learn of His goodness, and He chases away all the anxiety, all the fear, and all the doubts, we can have our lives back again. We can have our lives back again because He cares. God really cares about us. He cares about how we feel. He cares about what we do. He cares about whom we love, and who loves us. He helps us have the strength to face the day. It may be a hard day for us. We may have lots of struggles, but He will be there to help us when we need Him the most. Know that He is our present help in time of need. Do not forget who has the greater power. It is God who lives within us. We will be challenged by thoughts of fear, but it will back off each time we use God's words. Face our fears head-on, in Jesus's name.

Be thankful that because of Him, we have the power to put it to flight. Asking God's guidance in all we do is a comfort, knowing He will lead and guide us into all truth. He will teach us to listen to His words. Our minds are strong spirits, and we must use strong words to defeat our thinking. Remember that words are alive. If you never thought about words being alive, stop and think about words that have been spoken to you in the past. If they were encouraging words, they gave a lift to your life. If they were hurtful words, sometimes we never forget them. Sometimes it was a long time before we forgave others for those words.

Listening. We may even hear God say, "God is peace." When doubts and fears and anxieties come our way, we can say no! I will not listen to those negatives that would destroy my peace. I will repeat repeatedly, "God is peace." If God is peace, we do not need anything else. We do not need to listen to those other voices. Those other voices pull us down and keep us trapped. God is peace. We can go on our way knowing God does not give us a spirit of fear but of love and power and a sound mind. If the words we hear are not love, power, and a sound mind, we do not have to listen. We are not captive to those words. We can say, "Get behind me." I will not listen to those words because I know God is peace, and if I do not know that, I will ask God to help me to know that He is peace and will teach me. These words were not just made up by some person. These words are spirit. This is God's spirit living within us. He gave His life so He could live within us and give us peace. He did not give His life in vain. When we are raging inside, we say, "I cannot take it anymore. I am going to reach for something else for relief. I have to get relief." When we think we cannot take anymore, remember where our help is. We may say all other minds are coming against us. We may say that God does not care. "Where is God? I cannot see God. I cannot feel God. How do I really know He is there?" Because He has given us relief before, He has given us peace before, He has given us rest before. Wait on Him. He says those who wait upon the Lord will renew their strength. That is what we need: we need our strength renewed. Sometimes we feel so weak, so helpless, so out of place, and nobody cares. "But they that wait upon the Lord shall renew their strength; they shall mount up with wings as eagles; they shall run, and not be weary; and they shall walk, and not faint" (Isaiah 40:31). Teach me, Lord, to wait.

Talk to God. Our nerves can be so rattled that we do not want to hear anybody say a word. We cannot stand any loud sound, and we do not want anybody around. We do not want any problems to face us. We are at our wits' end! Then we call upon the name of the Lord, and He shall rescue us. He shall save us from our torments, our fears, our misgivings, and our agitation. Anything that would come against our being, God cares. For God is peace.

"Holy is His name, and greatly to be praised," is my sentiment.

Then God will give us peace. He will give us words. He may say, "Peace be still." He may say, "God is peace." He may say, "I come to make a way." God can talk. Talk to Him like you would a friend. You can even talk to Him easier than you can a friend. You know He understands.

He will know what we are saying. He believes us. He knows us. He knows what we are going to ask even before we ask. So, fear not! Fear not to talk to him. Fear not to ask for help. We need a life that we have never even had before. We can have that life when His words are written on our hearts and minds, and we will have learned of His goodness. We can go to the doctors, but we need to pray that they will get wisdom from God to help us. We need to believe God will give us wisdom and understanding as to what is right for us. God can put His arms around us and hold us until the storms pass. He will be there to help clean up the damage from the storms of life.

With God's Help, We Will Overcome. People say we can control these anxieties. "Just do it! You do not have to let your mind do that to you!" How we wish we could just do it. With God's Word, we can overcome. I kept a book close by, and I wrote down my thoughts and prayers. It was a lot of help. I could go back later and read what I had written. I could see progress when I needed to remind myself that God is peace. God is faithful and waiting to help me. His Word does not fail; it remains the same. If we heard His Word yesterday, it is still good today. One day at a time, we will be overcomers. We will reach that shining light at the end of the tunnel.

I found out my anxiety was caused by a medicine that was working against me. It took several trips and letters before my doctor would even consider that it may be the medicine. He suggested I see a psychologist for counseling. I tried to get an appointment, but I could not find one who would take my insurance. The anxiety was so captive that I was willing to do whatever I could to get help. The doctor later admitted it was the medicine. After he changed the medicine, I started to get better. I felt that it was the medicine from the beginning, but he would not hear me. Sometimes we know our bodies better than anyone else.

Even though it was the medicine, God's Word still came to my rescue and did what His Word was sent to do: bring peace. Anxiety is the same no matter the root cause and takes over our thinking. It is like fear: it does the same damage no matter where the fear comes from.

I know a person who is tempted to take extra pills when he is anxious. When the pills wear off, he is still left facing his anxiety, and besides, there is the danger of an overdose. He started to read God's Word, and when he was tempted to take extra pills, he would ask God to help him resist. He asked for help to put down the thoughts that were tempting him. He was captive to those thoughts only when he listened to them. Sometimes he resisted just five minutes at a time, until he would make it through the temptation. Each time he resisted he would gain faith that God would always be there for him if he asked Him.

The more we trust, the more we can trust. At first it is hard to believe something you cannot see. Before long you will be able to see and feel deliverance. Then no one can take that faith away because you see and feel it in your life.

Our help is in holding tight to the hand that will lead us out. No one can take that faith away as you experience His peace in your life.

Remember, our help is in holding tight to the hand that will lead us out.

46

In the Garden

Jesus's time had come. He had accomplished all the Father had ask Him to accomplish, while here on earth.

He had lived on this earth showing the whole world what it was like to be a Son of God. Fear and doubt and unbelief were keeping his children from believing that.
He had accomplished all except one thing.

Except one thing!

He had not given His life to forgive God's children of their sins of fear, doubt, and unbelief. The sins of God's children.

Go back and look at Adam and Eve. They did not believe their Father God. It started there and all down through the Old Testament fear, doubt and unbelief ruled. Those sins abound. It was prophesied in the old testament a savior would come and redeem God's children.

Jesus came. He was the light of the world.

As a young man it came time to give His life for all people. To cover their sins of fear, doubt, and unbelief. The sins that keep us from believing we are made in God's image and are His children.

He knew that day would come, and He knew the consequence.

His time had come!

Jesus, ask His disciples to watch while He went and prayed.

He went into the garden and prayed to His Father. Oh! How He prayed. He told His Father He did not think He would be able to give His life. Was not there some other way to redeem His children? He was afraid to face what lie ahead. Oh! The pain, the disgrace. The humiliation. The hatred and bitterness of His accusers. He felt it was more that He could bear. He went out to check on the disciples and they were asleep. Jesus asked them to watch for His accusers a little longer, while He went back to pray. Jesus needed more time to decide what He was going to do. He was still torn. He was still praying for another way.

He went back and prayed. His whole body was wrenching with pain of fear, and doubt, that he could do it. His sweat was as droplets of blood. Unbelief was right there at the door. All the weaknesses of the whole world lay on His breast. He felt in His body everything we will ever feel.

His Father saw His Son agonizing with what He had to do. God says, "Son, this is what you came to earth to do. To show the world what a Son of God is like, and to redeem my children back to me, so I can forgive them of all their sins. Son, only you can do this." Jesus said "I trust you Father. If there is not any other way then, not my will, but thy will be done." As His whole being was agonizing in pain. He trusted His Father who had never let Him down.

That day while in the garden; He had surrendered His life. There is where He won the battle before He was ever crucified. He put His life in God's hands.

You know that is where our battles are fought and won. Talking to God. Knowing Jesus died and arose again and lives. We have that same hope as we talk to our heavenly Father, and we put our life in His hands; knowing He knows best.

47

When the Spirit Speaks: Come, My Love

I am coming, I am coming. Don't you
hear the trumpet sound?
I am coming, I am coming to take My children home.
In the still of the night, or in the bright sunlight of day,
you can hear Gabriel's message clearing the way.
Come, My love. You have waited long.
Come rest from your labors and trials and tears.
Come, My love. I have peace to give.
Come, My love. Come and enter My rest. Your burdens
shall be lifted; your voice shall ring in praise.
Come, My love. Enter in today. There is rest for
the sin sick, the burdened and distressed.
Come, My love. See your family and friends.
They are all waiting with outstretched arms.
Waiting to hold you once again.
I come, My love! For you I come.
Come, My people. Come and see!
There is rest for the weary, rest in Me.
Come, if you are hungry. Come, come, please.
Come, take of My manna; your hunger shall cease.
I care when you fear. I care how you feel.
I care when you are hurting. I care when you succeed.

There is no power that can befall you.
No harm can come your way.
Come partake of My goodness. Have peace this day.

The Gospel of Peace

Printed in the United States
By Bookmasters